BE A
BELL RINGER

BE A
BELL RINGER

Elaine Cannon

Bookcraft
Salt Lake City, Utah

Library of Congress Catalog Card Number: 89–62193

ISBN 0–88494–710–6

2nd Printing, 1989

Printed in the United States of America

Contents

Introduction

A girl is only young and growing once in her life. You may be that girl at this time. Go for it!

Make life wonderful. Make it memorable for yourself and for others. Why not? What do you have to lose? Nothing! What do you have to gain? An even better you plus greater self-appreciation and gratitude to God for the gift of life. And you'll probably have a whole new address book full of friends!

Becoming is more exciting than static being. You are on your way with this book about bells and belles. Bells are such interesting collectables. And this is the season for them. They are our symbol, our excuse for helping you get where you want to be.

One hundred and twenty years ago someone else wanted to help girls; his dream has grown through the years and benefits you today. That special someone was Brigham Young, unique colonizer of a great part of the West and spiritual leader of the Latter-day Saints, as well. He rang a bell in more ways than one, and a whole new way of life for young women—a higher life of purpose and appropriateness—got under way.

During the hundredth anniversary of this event, Christine Knickerbocker was thirteen or fourteen years old and wrote a verse about bells. Little did she know then that she would grow up to be a president of her stake's Young Women organization during the rousing, bell-ringing 120th celebration. Here is that verse Christine wrote as a school girl:

Bells

Bells to wake one in the morn
Bells a horsecart to adorn

Bells to mark a burglar's fun
Bells to keep one on the run
Bells to hail a bright new year
Bells for showing someone's here
Bells for instruments may be
Bells a change in class decree
But my favorite bell that peals
Is that calling me to meals

Now we go from the perspective of a thirteen-year-old to the familiar lines of a famous poet, Edgar Allan Poe, to get you in the bell-ringing, life-charming, happy-time frame of mind to take hold of your youth and grow with it!

The Bells

I

Hear the sledges with the bells—
Silver bells!
What a world of merriment their melody foretells!
How they tinkle, tinkle, tinkle,
In the icy air of night!
While the stars that oversprinkle
All the heavens, seem to twinkle
With a crystalline delight;
Keeping time, time, time,
In a sort of Runic rhyme,
To the tintinnabulation that so musically wells
From the bells, bells, bells, bells,
Bells, bells, bells—
From the jingling and the tinkling of the bells.

II

Hear the mellow wedding bells—
Golden Bells!
What a world of happiness their harmony foretells!
Through the balmy air of night

How they ring out their delight!—
From the molten-golden notes,
   And all in tune,
What a liquid ditty floats
To the turtle-dove that listens, while she gloats
   On the moon!
Oh, from out the sounding cells,
What a gush of euphony voluminously wells!
   How it swells!
   How it dwells
On the Future!—how it tells
Of the rapture that impels
To the swinging and the ringing
   Of the bells, bells, bells—
   Of the bells, bells, bells, bells,
      Bells, bells, bells—
To the rhyming and the chiming of the bells!

· · · · · · · · · · · ·

(*Treasury of the Familiar*, ed. Ralph L. Woods [New York: MacMillian Co., 1959], p. 612.)

So vices brag,
but virtue bears the bell.

—George Gascoigne

Bells, Belles, and Bell Ringers

This is a book about bells and belles.

It is a book about your being someone who can make a difference in your particular surroundings. You do it by being a bell ringer.

A bell ringer is someone who sounds a call, issues a warning, rings a signal, or chimes a time. A bell ringer, you see, makes things happen.

Brigham Young was a bell ringer.

All the young women of The Church of Jesus Christ of Latter-day Saints owe Brigham Young a debt of gratitude for getting a very great thing going—the worldwide organization they belong to. Maybe you have heard the story before, but it bears telling again because it all started with the ring of a bell.

One evening in late November in 1869, Brigham Young sat at his desk after dinner, listening to his many daughters giggle, swish their ruffled petticoats, and rustle their billowing dresses as they moved through the house.

You see, he had been worrying about his daughters. As President of the Church and a prophet of God, when Brigham Young worried, he prayed and then waited upon God for direction.

One evening his spirit received an answer to the nagging question about his charming but frivolous daughters. He was told to advise them to change their values, to retrench, to cut off their life from or to turn away from the shallow appearance and worldly behavior that they were imitating. They were daughters of God, and they also were daughters of the current Church president—people looked upon them as models.

With a prayer in his heart, President Young—who was a concerned and loving father as well as the President and prophet—rose from his plush chair and solemnly walked from his office to the adjoining Lion House. There he took the prayer bell from its niche in the wall. He stood in the doorway to the parlor and rang the bell eight times, very deliberately. It was the signal for the family to gather for evening prayer.

In they came—laughing, chattering, making social plans, and sharing ideas for the latest fashions. They were, of course, totally unaware that tonight was going to be different. Oh, they were in for a surprise!

But first there was family prayer. Brigham Young asked for God's blessings on the nation, still reeling from President Abraham Lincoln's assassination, and on the loyal laborers who were on a precarious errand to bring mammoth granite slabs from the mountains to the valley for the building of the temple. He prayed for himself as leader of a courageous but lively people, that he might guide the Saints in paths of righteousness according to the Lord's will.

The prayer ended at last, and the younger daughters and sons were dismissed. He studied the beautiful, familiar faces of those who remained. How dearly he loved them! He wanted the best for them. He wanted them to live close to the Lord and be ready to help in the work of proselyting and teaching others to do God's will. He did not want to lose even *one* of his posterity to the adversary's wiles.

Then Brigham Young looked into each upturned, waiting face, and took courage to say the words that would change their lives.

"All Israel are looking to my family and watching the example set by my wives and children. For this reason I desire to organize my own family first into a society for the promotion of habits of order, thrift, industry, and charity, and, above all things, I desire them to retrench from their extravagance in dress, in eating, and even in speech. The time has come when the sisters must agree to give up their follies of dress and cultivate a modest apparel, a meek deportment, and to set an example before the people of the world worthy of imitation. . . . Our daughters are following the vain and foolish fashions of the world. I want you to set your own fashions. Let your apparel be neat and comely, and the workmanship of your own hands. Wear the good cloth manufactured in our own mills, and cease to build up the merchant who sends your money out of the Territory for fine clothes made in the East. . . . I should like you to get up your own fashions, and set the style for all the rest of the world who desire sensible and comely fashions to follow. I want my daughters to learn to work and to do it, not to spend their time for naught; for our time is all the capital God has given us, and if we waste that, we are bankrupt indeed. . . . There is need for the young daughters of Israel to get a living testimony of truth. . . . I wish our girls to obtain a knowledge of the Gospel for themselves. For this purpose I desire to establish this organization and want my family to lead out in the great work. I have always been willing to give my children all the advantages of education and schooling possible to obtain. But I want them to appreciate those advantages and not to squander their opportunities.

"We are about to organize a Retrenchment Association, which I want you all to join. . . . Retrench in everything that is bad and worthless, and improve in everything that is good and beautiful, . . . not to make yourselves unhappy, but to live so that you may be truly happy in this life and the life to come."

That was the beginning. In spite of natural youthful vanities and keen interest in worldly frivolities, the girls knew that their loving father was a prophet and had their best interests at heart. He was truly guided by God; they had seen this in so many ways.

As the days and weeks unfolded, they caught the spirit of the new movement and became *cooperative* members of the Young Ladies Department of the Cooperative Retrenchment Association striving to be "worthy of imitation." ("A Century of Sisterhood—Chronological Collage 1869–1960," LDS Church Historical Department, Young Women, pp. 8–10.)

Saved by the bell!

Well, that was then. But what about now? What about you?

If you were to tour the Lion House in Salt Lake City, you would see a handsome brass plaque mounted near the entrance, marking it historically as the place where Brigham Young rang the bell that has affected young women across the world.

In the Lion House also, you would see a beautiful handmade doll which the Young Women organization commissioned Inez Stanton to make in 1980. This was done so that succeeding generations of young women could see the details of the official Retrenchment Association costume.

For many years the Young Women General Board gave a bell to those who spoke to us or whom we wanted especially to honor. It was a small replica of the black handled brass bell used by Brigham Young to call his daughters together to form the Retrenchment Association. This, as you now know, became the Young Women organization of The Church of Jesus Christ of Latter-day Saints. You may want such a bell in your own collection. As members of the Young Women organization today, you aren't required to wear pantaloons and quaint frocks with high necks and long sleeves. However, your ideals are expected to be as high. Prophets have spoken to you, too!

Standards of behavior are essentially the same. You are supposed to be exemplary and "worthy of imitation" in how you look and how you think, in your values, your goals, your worship, and your obedience to God. You are to do good deeds, think pure thoughts, and develop yourself so that you *can* make a fine difference in the world.

You belles must be bell ringers!

This book is to help you—to give you some ideas and show you how.

They tune like bells,
and want but hanging.

—Thomas Adams

All About Bells

Once upon a time there was a fine community of small, plump, and juicy looking mice. They were ordinary gray field mice who liked to come into the big house in the winter where it was warm; there was room enough to hide the whole exploding collection of big and little gray mice. There were also delicious crumbs on the floor.

Now, though these mice were quick creatures and could scurry through life rather easily, for the most part, as summer turned into fall they learned through personal tragedy that they had a very big, furry problem.

There was a cat in the big house.

This cat was bigger than they were, of course. He also was faster. He had great agility and could leap and pounce and prey upon the little gray mice. He could wipe out a whole neighborhood of mice with the flick of a whisker, or so it seemed. And what's more, he took great sport in doing it. He was absolutely stealthy, silent, and therefore totally surprising in his attacks.

Talk about horror stories!

Well, the Mouse Community Council hastily met to address their situation.

After much discussion and after many proposed and abandoned solutions to this life-and-death problem, the mice determined that it would help matters considerably if they at least knew when the cat was in the area. They needed a warning soon enough to safely gather in their mouseketeers and hide.

It was agreed: A bell should be tied to the cat.

A great idea.

Mouse scouts had located a bell in a child's toy basket in the big house. A piece of floss from the sewing room floor would do nicely as a tie. Now, who would tie the bell on the cat? Who had the courage, the daring, the unselfishness, the unmitigated nerve to risk the deed?

If you have read up on your fairy tales and true-to-life stories, you know that here is exactly the point where the problem was left—at least in my memory. Not one mouse would volunteer or even respond to a direct command to tie the bell on the cat. Risking one's own life to save another's is sometimes a foolish way to behave, even for a mouse.

Well, that community of mice is long since gone. But then so is the cat, thanks to the ravages of time—and unfriendly dogs. Since then the phrase "tieing the bell on the cat" has been used to describe risk and challenge.

Isn't it sobering, though, to think how many mice might have been saved by a bell?

Saved by the bell!

This is what often is said when a boxer has been knocked down for the count which could end the fight and the time bell rings for that round before the count is finished. The boxer is given a chance to revive before he goes in for the next round. He is "saved by the bell."

This phrase has come to mean that something happens *just in time* to give you another chance, preserve your life, guard your reputation, straighten you out, turn you around, cause you to repent or behave differently, or to get out of a questionable, threatening, unwholesome situation.

The young women of Brigham Young's day were saved by a bell, which the prophet rang. They were warned and instructed. A commitment was exacted from them. This is happening to you today. But what bell? Rung by whom? How? And why?

Before we answer those questions and talk about *your* life, let's talk all about bells for a few minutes.

Bells are practical. They are symbolic. They are useful in countless ways. If you study a dictionary, encyclopedia, and thesaurus, for example, you will learn interesting things about bells that will tie into your life.

Being a student, you are familiar with how such resource books convey information. We'll follow that same format here as we share our research from many sources about how bells began, how they are made and used, and what meanings have been given them over the centuries. Even that little mouse story was retold to stir up your interest in an exciting idea that bells can make your life better.

Definition

Bell: A hollow object of resonant material that vibrates and gives forth a ringing sound when struck. The word *bell* comes from Anglo-Saxon *bellan,* meaning "to bellow." In other languages the word *bell* is *cloche* (French), *Glocke* (German), *Klok* (Dutch), and *clooca* (Middle Latin). The

English cognate of these words is *clock*, an item that rings the hour.

The science and art of bells and bell ringing is called campanology, a word derived from the Italian *campana,* meaning "bell."

Origin of bells

According to the *Encyclopedia Americana*, the history of the ringing bell begins with the Bronze Age. "Staves, dishes, pots of hammered metal and cast bronze all have a certain ring, and it may easily be conceived that the more or less resonant tone of such vessels was known and utilized as a form of amusement and as a signal."

But even before that, a kind of beginning bell was noted. A flat clay disk or small stone, and finally a cast coin, was secured to another such disk by a twisted reed or a thong. When this "rattle" was hung from a limb or tent pole, the wind would catch it and hit the disks upon each other, making a pleasant tinkling sound. Perhaps the obvious benefits came when this contraption was discovered to attract the attention of a baby playing beneath or of a family within a dwelling. Then ingenious man found ways to make a bigger instrument whose sound would carry long distances or be resonant enough to command the people's response in time of crisis, announcement, or important ceremony. And finally they learned how to shape a bell into a specific tone.

How bells are made

Today bells are made using a combination of science and craftsmanship. The size of the bell must be calculated according to its desired tone when rung. This is governed by the width, height, and thickness of the metal. To state it simply, two molds are made—an inner or "core" mold and an outer one called the "cope," which is first made as a dummy bell in clay to the exact size the finished bell is to be. This is covered with a thin coat of beeswax. At this time any ornamentation or inscription is added. Many coats are used to build up the clay before it is baked. The space between the "cope" and the "core" is at last filled with a specific mix of molten metal. When the casting is cooled, the mold is removed, and the bell is cleaned and prepared for tuning. It is the musical quality called a "minor third" that distinguishes the bell from all other musical instruments and gives it its appealing, plaintive sound.

Not every bell's construction is a success story. One of the world's largest bells is in the Kremlin in Moscow and has never been heard. When it was first struck by the clapper, a big piece broke from it due to a fault in casting in 1733; thus, though it is a mighty attraction, it is never rung.

The famous Liberty Bell of America is silent, too. It has a circumference of 142 inches compared to the Czar Kolokol bell's *diameter* of 272 inches. The Russian bell is obviously much bigger. But neither bell really fulfilled the measure of its creation. The Liberty Bell was cast in 1752; it also broke before its tone could be heard. When it was hung up to try the sound, the first stroke of the clapper cracked it. It was recast but broke again while being tolled during the funeral procession of Chief Justice John Marshall in 1835, and again when it was last rung on George Washington's birthday in 1846.

This beloved bell, a symbol of freedom and liberty, was widely associated with antislavery. It carries the biblical inscription, "Proclaim liberty throughout the land unto all the inhabitants thereof." It is now the main attraction of Independence National Historical Park in Philadelphia, Pennsylvania.

Bells, like belles, are nice to look at, but are better if they are also useful. Remember the words of the song, "A bell isn't a bell until you ring it, and love isn't love until you give it away." In other words, when we talk about bells and about your being a belle who is a bell ringer, it is better if you are than if you are not!

Uses of bells

The uses of bells are numerous and so varied that there is no possible way to make a complete listing here. Historically bells have always been used in connection with the time of day, religious rites, or a call to worship or for town counsel; for a call to arms or dinner at the cabin; to hail a success or mourn a defeat; for warnings, fire, flood, or Indian attack; for opening doors and sealing them shut, as in a vault; for funerals, celebrations, weddings, birth of royalty, the end of a work day, or the beginning of the Sabbath; for shore safety (as bells tied to a buoy near a dangerous coastline); and also for musical events, such as operas and symphonies.

Bell ringers

Professional musicians have arranged classical and popular music for bells and played them in scale as they would use traditional musical instruments. Bell ringers like these need skill and practice and are highly regarded. Sometimes a bell ringer is known by a fun-sounding name —tintinnabulator. A bell ringer is also one who pulls a cord that rings the bell sounding a warning or signal.

Bellwether

This is the practice of "belling" the leader of a flock; it also means one who takes the lead or initiative, an indicator of trends.

In *Roget's Thesaurus* we learn that a bellwether is a leader, conductor, header, precentor, coryphaeus; pacemaker, pacesetter; bell mare, standard bearer; forerunner, ringleader.

Belle

A belle is a popular and attractive girl or woman; especially a girl or woman whose charm and beauty makes her popular.

Are you beginning to get the message? Bells, belles, and bell ringers (or tintinnabulators) are very important people in today's world. Especially in your particular world. Youth need warning. Youth need a signal to follow. Youth need a call to worship, a bell ringer to alert them, and a bellwether to indicate trends—wholesome and otherwise. And youth need a chance to celebrate in a mighty statement of commitment to successfully perform God's will.

So what the world needs is a courageous and wise, obedient and caring young woman—better yet, a massive group of them in this highly populated, misguided world—to be bell ringers. We need charming and credible bellwethers, examples, and leaders.

And that is where *you* come in!

Bells [and belles] are
Music's laughter.

—Thomas Hood

About Belles and You

You've learned all about bells; now let's talk all about belles—about you and your friends.

Do you recall the definition of *belle* that we included in the last chapter? Webster said that when a girl was popular because of her charm and beauty, she was a belle. You know, "Belle of the ball." Some dream!

It can happen to you.

In today's world beauty can be arranged, bought at a price. Even charm and poise can be acquired through training and practice. "Polishing people" agencies multiply regularly across America. Yes, it can happen to you if this is the direction for your life.

Maybe you want to become something a little more lasting than the belle of the prom or ball. Maybe you are more interested in scholarship, fitness, sports, volunteerism, service projects, crafts, or professional development in an area such as music or dance.

When you make a thorough study of yourself you learn this, at least: what you have is what you get to work with.

Remember the story of the brother and sister getting ready for church? The scrunch on the bathroom was something fierce. Sister's hair wasn't turning out right. So she began to snipe at her brother jealously. As he shut off his blow drier and walked forth looking like Mr. Wonderful, she complained, "It isn't fair! You got the curly hair and the straight nose."

"Ah, come on, Sis," he teased. "Everything comes out equal. Look at it this way—you got the straight hair and curly nose!"

Brothers.

Still he was right in his way.

It's true, though, that what you now are is where you have to start. So it seems wise to start where you are, and, as you keep at it, life has a way of giving you what you deserve in the long run. That is a kind of equality.

Remember, what you have is what you *can* work with. And what amazing things you can do with yourself, your looks, your character, your mind, your personality, your personal appeal or charm!

You can be a bell ringer: you can make things happen. What *do* you want to make happen for yourself or others? What bells do you want to ring?

What do you want to become?

What kind of person do you want to be?

What *do* you have to work with? Let's go back to the basics and consider that all-important matter of what is yours:

1. You are a daughter of God.
2. You are a sister to the Savior.

3. You are heir to certain biological and environmental influences—thanks to your parents.
4. You have a unique spirit.

Here is a verse of truth. Think upon it a moment:

> Before this world was
> And after it's through,
> Always you have been
> And always will be YOU!

Who are you, then? You'll fill in the details about what your name is, who your parents and family members are, where you live and go to school; your birthdate, food preferences, music and book preferences, leisure preferences, favorite subjects, scripture reading goals, personal progress, talents, and so on.

Those are your particular personal details. Let's consider the two or three basic elements that you and your bell ringing belle friends have in common.

You are a daughter of God

You have the spark of the divine in you. Whatever you do or don't do won't change this fact. Your spirit was marvelously created in the premortal world by your Heavenly Father and your Heavenly Mother. We don't know much about this, but if you ask in prayer, the Holy Ghost will witness to your spirit of your divine beginnings.

Heavenly Father wants you to succeed and to be happy. He wants you to come home to him after you have lived and learned enough to dwell in his presence.

Marcie was the oldest of ten children. She was twelve when her mother died of cancer. That threw a great load on her shoulders for a time—a lot of around-the-house work, all those children, and a new baby besides. Her dad thought she did a great job. In fact, he was worried about her turning into a Cinderella slave to her family, and so he began looking for another wife to be mother to the family.

When two families mix, adjustments can be difficult for everyone. When the new mother came into Marcie's home, there was trouble at once. She and Marcie didn't hit it off. Marcie's dad couldn't take sides with either one against the other, now could he? It was "push against shove" for Marcie.

Marcie felt that she wasn't valued or loved. She withdrew from the family, struggled with herself, and limped into her fifteenth year in real trouble as a young sinner. New friends hovered around her when she led the pack in thinking up exotic, shameful, and daring things to try.

When she found out that she was going to have a baby, she was heartsick. She knew about babies and the breath of heaven they brought with them to earth. She'd welcomed so many brothers and sisters when Mother was alive. Now here she was bringing one into the world with no home, and she'd hardly had time to be young herself.

Suddenly Marcie needed God again.

Suddenly she wanted him to be there for her. It had been so long since she had prayed. God went out of her life when she withdrew from her family and each night began begging friends to let her "stay over" with them. That's when all the foolishness began.

One day Marcie walked alone up the foothills of the mountains behind her school. She selected a spot to be her Sacred Grove. Then she sat down because somehow she felt self-conscious and silly kneeling. Then she put her arms around her knees, with her head down over them. Soon her burdens weighed heavy upon her heart and she began to cry.

She cried for a long time until she was emotionally exhausted. She cried for all that now was going to be and all that never could be again. When at last she grew quiet in body and spirit, she whispered gently toward heaven, "Oh, Heavenly Father, if you are still there, help me! Help me! I'm Marcie and I am ready for you. Are you ready for me? I'm in a mess. I have no one. I need someone. I don't know what to do."

Marcie did not see God, as Joseph Smith had done in his Sacred Grove. But Marcie *knew* God in that hour. The Spirit of Heavenly Father flooded over her. Her mind cleared to receive inspiration about what she must do to right her wrong and move forward.

She knew she was loved and known to her Heavenly Father. She knew she would be helped and blessed and forgiven by the Savior. She knew, too, that she could be helped but she had a hard path still to walk. She was thankful that God would be there to help.

You are a daughter of God and he loves you more than you can ever imagine. Parents truly love their children. Earthly parents still have a lot to learn and may not be able to show love as each child would like it to be shown. But our Heavenly Father is different. He is great, perfect, in charge, and loves you no matter what. Because he abides in the eternal laws according to justice, he has his ways of showing love. Let him! Turn to him.

It made all the difference to Marcie, and it will to you, too.

You see, when you know that you truly are a daughter of God, you understand why the way you live is so critically important and why there are so many people (like me) trying to love, write, teach, preach, and help you make it through life's challenges. That is why the scriptures are full of the good news that God wants you to draw close to him so he can draw close to you.

Sing that song again, sing and believe the words, "I am a child of God . . ." If you are ready for heavier support, you can prove this truth by scripture study and the words of every latter-day prophet on the subject.

Being a child of God means that you are related to Heavenly Father in a special way. And you are loved as a dear family member.

Being a child of God means that you are heir to eternal and divine traits.

Being a child in Heavenly Father's eternal family means that you should try to live and be like your exemplary parents.

Being a child of God means that you are scheduled to go "home" to heaven some day.

That's the grand plan of life.

You are a spiritual sister to Jesus

Being a child of God means that Jesus is your elder brother as well as your Savior. It also means that spiritually you are a sister to your mother and father. Think upon that! They just came to earth earlier than you, with a special assignment concerning you.

Being a little sister to Jesus clarifies your eternal and spiritual position. Now to get through life successfully you become a member of The Church of Jesus Christ of Latter-day Saints, which he has set up and through which you can learn, serve, and grow more like Jesus. He is the perfect example. And Jesus will bless you. Keep close to him. Let him bless you along the way. Try to always remember him and keep his commandments, which he has given to help you so that you may always have his Spirit with you.

Nothing is impossible for you, because of Jesus.

You are a child of your earthly parents

You are heir to certain biological influences from your particular mother and father and a long list of ancestors.

You are heir to certain environmental influences from places and people you live with. The way they speak and feel about things rubs off.

You are unique

You may be Daddy's little girl but in many ways you are also captain of your own soul. That may be mind boggling, but it is true. It is one of life's best things to learn. You are different from anyone else on earth, according to God's creation! You are in charge, responsible, answerable for your choices—for your life.

There are many people, programs, procedures, and principles to help you through life. However, you choose how you act and react to
—what happens to you;
—what you are taught;
—when you are burdened or abused;
—how you are treated; and
—where you are placed.
You also choose
—whom you relate to;
—with whom you live, work, worship, study, compete, serve, and even double date;
—with whom you are friends; and
—where you live and what your own quarters are like.
Your responses to such things are influenced by what knowledge and wisdom you have gained about who you are, your relationship to God, and what you have come to understand about the purpose and plan of life.

Let's go over it one more time:

You are a daughter of God.

You are a sister to the Savior.

You are heir to biological and environmental influences (genes and things).

You are unique. The eternal spirit within you influences your responses.

Here is a bit of verse to commit to memory and to reach back into your secret heart to understand:

Baby Picture

So You were I . . .
Somehow
I can't think thru
To that forgotten time
When I was You.
Could your clear eyes
Read
What is in my own,
Would You
Feel disappointment
At the Me
To which
You've grown?

(Amy Atwater, in *The American Album of Poetry*, comp. Ted Malone [Chicago: Rodgeheaver, Hall-Mack Co., 1938], p. 92.)

For these bells have been anointed, . . .

—*Henry Wadsworth Longfellow*

CHAPTER

Blessings and Bell Ringers

Girls in Brigham Young's day—like the girls who answered the ring of Brigham's bell—had names such as Dora, Sadie, Phoebe, Henrietta, Hannah, Alice, Zina, Mary Isabella, Elmina, Martha, Carlie, Lina, Lona, Lucy, and Libby.

Girls today have names such as Hilary, Hailey, Heather, Jessica, Janna, Jennifer, Joanna, Jane, Abigail, Annie, Emily, Egan, Erin, Tiffany, Stephanie, Loralee, Catherine, Kristine, Kaline, Camilla, and Kate.

You probably have a pretty name, too. Whatever your name is, your Father in Heaven knows you by it. But he knows you by more than your name. He's known you always and forever. He has unique and special blessings in store for you. He has a particular work for you to do.

Your job is to find out about these things and make them happen.

Have you made arrangements yet to find out what your Heavenly Father has to say especially to you? There's a way to find out: it's called a patriarchal blessing.

President Harold B. Lee stood in his home ward to bear his testimony, and he told of attending a funeral that very week where the grown children of the deceased mother planned and participated in the funeral. A daughter gave some of her mother's life history. Then a son paid tribute to his mother and closed by saying, "Now I would like to tell you what the Lord had to say to our mother." He read a paragraph from her patriarchal blessing. President Lee asked the congregation to ask themselves if they had the faith to believe that God speaks to us through the patriarchs who lay hands upon our heads to give us blessings especially for us from Heavenly Father. He asked how many believed that the Lord does speak to us through the patriarchs regarding our mission on earth.

It is something to think about.

It may be that you will want to get your own patriarchal blessing. It can be a guide and a comfort. It is a sacred, sobering, spiritual experience to have such a blessing and to try to live worthy of its fulfillment.

As a Church we have the priesthood and authority through which such blessings are given. As descendants of Abraham of Old Testament times, we are entitled to all the blessings promised him and his posterity. So we can all receive promises of similar blessings in our lives. But there are other things that we should know about ourselves. A patriarchal blessing can reveal some of these things.

For example, do you know that when you have a patriarchal blessing, you can learn your lineage? Are you from the tribe of Ephraim, Manasseh, Dan? Can you discern what you should guard against? Also, what should you prepare for? What can you hope to accomplish in your lifetime? How and where can you best serve? What of your own posterity? What special mission is yours?

If you live true and faithful, you can learn much about yourself through a patriarchal blessing given by proper authority under appropriate circumstances. This blessing will be recorded and then stored in the archives of The Church of Jesus Christ of Latter-day Saints. A copy will be sent to you. Hold it safe. Keep it sacred. Read it frequently, especially if you have choices to make. Be private about the contents—this is for *you.*

Patriarchal blessings were given to people in olden days, too. It can be helpful to you to read scriptural accounts of various kinds of blessings given through the ages and then note the outcome of lives so blessed or the fulfillment of the blessings.

Grandfathers today, preparing to move on into the next world, have been known to gather their families about them, and, as the family patriarch, give a father's blessing. In ancient times, the blessing old father Jacob gave his grandsons (the sons of Joseph of Egypt) just before he died was remarkable.

The scripture says that "guiding his hands wittingly," Jacob placed his right hand upon the head of Ephraim, who was the younger, and crossed his left hand over to Manasseh's head, who was the first born and by tradition should have received his father's right hand upon his head. Then Jacob said, "God, before whom my fathers Abraham and Isaac did walk, the God which led me all my life long unto this day, . . . bless the lads; and let my name be named on them, and the name of my fathers Abraham and Isaac; and let them grow into a multitude in the midst of the earth."

The blessing and prediction was made by Jacob that the younger brother, Ephraim, "shall be greater . . . and his seed shall become a multitude of nations." You can read about this in Genesis 48:4–20 in your Old Testament.

Jacob then went on to bless each of his twelve sons and point out the paths of their future. We read, "All these are the twelve tribes of Israel: and this is it that their father spake unto them, and blessed them; every one according to his blessing he blessed them" (Genesis 49:28).

If you want some fascinating reading on this subject, turn to Genesis 49 and note the kinds of promises and predictions made in that day by Jacob regarding these now famous twelve tribes of Israel.

Lehi as well gathered his grandchildren around him to bless them before he died. The blessing he gave the sons and daughters of Laman, for example, is recorded in the Book of Mormon: "Wherefore, if ye are cursed, behold, I leave my blessing upon you, that the cursing may be taken from you and be answered upon the heads of your parents. Wherefore, *because of my blessing* the Lord God will not suffer that ye shall perish; wherefore, he will be merciful unto you and unto your seed forever." (2 Nephi 4:6–7; italics added.)

Today we are seeing the fulfillment of that blessing as Lamanite families come into the Church, grow in the gospel, fill missions, hold the priesthood, and contribute positively to society.

Choosing a wife was an important step in biblical times just as it is today. Yet how many young men today receive a father's blessing before choosing an eternal mate? I pray that you will have the great comfort of a father's blessing when you marry. Girls, I pray that you will have the comfort of a father's blessing the day before you get married, as well, and a blessing as you prepare to give birth to each baby you receive into your family.

When Abraham and Isaac decided it was time for Isaac to have a wife, a servant was sent forth to Nahor with the promise that an angel of the Lord would go before him all the way. The servant was to ask for water of the first virgin who came to the well. If she answered that she would also draw water for the camels, this was the girl the Lord had chosen for Isaac. And Rebekah was this girl. She took the servant home to her family so he could explain what was wanted.

Before Rebekah left home to join Isaac as his wife, she was given a blessing. These are some of the words spoken to her: "Thou art our sister, be thou the mother of thousands of millions, and let thy seed possess the gate of those which hate them" (Genesis 24:60; see entire chapter for the complete story).

Rebekah and Isaac had a son named Jacob (we told you how he grew into a grandfather who gave his posterity blessings), and when it was time for him to take a wife, his father, Isaac, gave him a blessing: "Thou shalt not take a wife of the daughters of Canaan"; and he told him where to go, who to find, and how to choose, plus this comforting promise: "Thou mayest inherit the land wherein thou art a stranger, which God gave unto Abraham."

I know a family in which the father gave a blessing to one of his children who had been elected to a student body office at high school. This is a family to whom living the gospel is a blessing itself and a personal privilege as well as a duty. Here was a chance for a family member to be a light unto the students of this particular high school. With the father's blessing he was given extra and important strengths, and he felt sustained in his new opportunity.

You may have a patriarchal blessing from a Church patriarch only once. It provides a unique template for your life. Along the way as opportunities and needs surface, you can turn to your father or the elders of the Church for further personal blessings.

There are fine examples of fathers giving blessings to their sons and daughters in the scriptures. In 1 Chronicles 29:22 we learn that when Solomon was to become king after his father David, he was anointed unto the Lord in a special ceremony of "great gladness." But before that public ceremony, King David gave his son a father's blessing in which Solomon was counseled to "be strong and of good courage, and do it: fear not, nor be dismayed: for the Lord God . . . will be with thee; he will not fail thee nor forsake thee, until thou hast finished all the work for the service of the house of the Lord."

A beautiful lesson about church calls and service in life for youth today can be learned by reading about the appointments of both Saul and David and the blessings given to them. The Lord didn't know these boys for the great deeds they had already done, for they had not done any. David was a mere shepherd boy with little experience. Saul was a Benjamite, a member of the smallest tribe of Israel; as he told the prophet Samuel, "My family is the least of all the families of the tribe of Benjamin . . . , wherefore then speakest thou so to me?" These two were chosen for their potential and promise.

In 1 Samuel 10:1–9 we learn that Samuel "took a vial of oil, and poured it upon his [Saul's] head, and kissed him, and said, Is it not because the Lord hath anointed thee to be captain over his inheritance?" Then Samuel told Saul of signs that would occur when he left, including his meeting a company of prophets. "And the Spirit of the Lord will come upon thee," continued Samuel, "and thou shalt prophesy with them, and shalt be turned into another man."

And it came to pass. It happened!

We can turn into other people—greater selves, winners, bell ringers—as we use our patriarchal blessing to motivate and guide and strengthen us to be what God intends us to be, and needs us to be.

Sometimes the patriarch is inspired to reveal sacred information. It is then recorded to await fulfillment. This was the case when President George Albert Smith was thirteen years old and very ill. The family felt he wouldn't live very long because he was sickly. At this time a patriarch gave a blessing to young George Albert. Among other things it said, "Thou shalt be wrapt in the visions of the heavens, and thou shalt be clothed with salvation as with a garment, for thou art destined to become a mighty man before the Lord, for thou shalt become a mighty apostle in the Church and kingdom of God upon the Earth, for none of thy father's family shall have more power with God than thou shalt have, for none shall excel thee."

This was a staggering promise to say to young George Albert—unless the patriarch were truly inspired to do so. You see, the father of the sickly child was John Henry Smith, Second Counselor to President Joseph F. Smith. George's grandfather was George A. Smith, who had been First Counselor in the First Presidency to Brigham Young. So if this blessing were to be fulfilled—"none shall excel thee"—George Albert Smith would have to become President of the Church someday. This indeed came to pass, too.

Blessings are a vital part of our lives—of your life. We ask for blessings. God has promised them to us if we keep his commandments. We should count on them and thank God for them.

The faithful children of our Heavenly Father since the beginning have enjoyed a richer life when they have called upon God for guidance and enlightenment.

Take time to prepare yourself spiritually—strengthening your faith—to have a patriarchal blessing. You will learn in the sweetest way what God has to say to you about you and your life.

Once you understand more clearly who you are, what you are here on earth to do, what gifts you have been given for accomplishing your mission on earth, you can move forward with more direction and confidence to be a bell ringer, a winner, a person who sets the example, sounds the signal, and makes a difference in the quality of life.

Now, let me share with you a page or two from my life

story, published under the title *Summer of My Content.* This selection deals with receiving my own patriarchal blessing, by which I have tried to live all the rest of my life.

At seventeen I felt very grown-up. I was about to have my patriarchal blessing. There had been fasting and prayer and deep discussions about the meaning of it all with my parents and my boyfriend. It was summer's time of roses, mock orange, and honeysuckle sweetening the air. Everything was at its best and I wanted to be.

The night before my appointment with Patriarch Charles Jones I felt a strong need to gather myself together with Heavenly Father. I went quickly out the screened door and stood there for a time listening to the summers of my youth sift by on the night song of the crickets.

Then I felt once again the pull of the stars. Shyly at first I lay down on my back on prickly grass as I had done so often as a child. Once again I took a deep breath and dared to turn my face directly up, skyward. Breathing deeply I recited Millay's phrase I'd memorized in English—"O world, I cannot hold thee close enough."

Once again I studied the heavens, finding the familiar constellations, getting placement with the North Star. Then finally, the mind-stretching, soul-searing experience of feeling "lifted" into the universe, almost into the presence of God, set my heart pounding.

My prayers that night got through. The witness of the Spirit to my spirit was that God lives and cares and is mindful of little me. I was warmed to tears.

That was the green summer—the beginning of my trying to make decisions according to God's will for me and committing myself to a way of life that would ensure fulfillment of his sacred promises.

My name was Elaine Winifred Anderson at that time. In grade school for five years I sat next to a girl named Winnifred Elaine Clive. We thought that was some magic arrangement, because the names were quite unusual! I went through college as a close friend to a girl named Elaine Anderson. On paper we were always getting confused for each other. We both ran for various student offices and had stories in the school paper. Naturally we won elections each time we were nominated because with our combined friends we had double the votes.

Even though my name wasn't unique, I came to know that Heavenly Father knew me for myself, loved me for myself, had things for me to do that were different from what he had in mind for those friends of mine with similar names.

You can know this about yourself as well. You may need to find a time and place very soon to talk this all over with God.

Think about these things:

1. Has your name been placed on the records of the Church? Did your father, grandfather, or other Melchizedek Priesthood bearer give you a blessing when you were given a name?
2. Do you have a birth certificate? Is your name correctly filled out on it?
3. Have you certificates of baptism and confirmation? Is your name correct on them?
4. Have you had your patriarchal blessing yet?
5. Are your sacred, personal records and blessings in a safe place where you can refer to them easily?

Whatever your name is, as we said in the beginning of this chapter, Heavenly Father and the Lord Jesus Christ know you as *you*. Now your job is to come to know them and be willing to learn to do what they want you to do. When you know the will of God for you and you learn to follow it, *it will be well for you!*

They may ring their bells now;
Before long they will be wringing their hands.

—Sir Robert Walpole

About Boys

Boys are important. Especially to girls.

Boys are one of the real bonuses in life for most girls.

Boys come in assorted sizes, shapes, colors, abilities, and bankrolls or connections, so to speak.

Boys can charm, disarm, warm, and alarm. They can even harm a girl.

No doubt about it, a girl like you needs your wits about you around boys. Otherwise you can blow all your young years and maybe put a terrible thorn in your entire life.

We're talking about sex here.

Let's get one thing out of the way—when it comes to boys and girls, male and female, men and women, guys and gals, or any other combination, sex is a sin unless you are legally and lawfully married.

Anyone who tells you otherwise is lying, or is foolish, or is certainly pitifully misguided. And they are leading you astray.

Don't listen—they are in defiance of God's rules and purposes. If you listen to such opinion and take part in such action, *you* will be a sinner against God.

Let's clear up a point about sin.

Sin is forbidden by God because it is hurtful. It is not hurtful because it is forbidden. The best counsel you can get is not to sin.

You may have heard how President Spencer W. Kimball always told the Saints, "Do it!" He wanted people to get going with their good lives and important duties. No more procrastination.

When I was serving as general president of the Young Women of The Church of Jesus Christ of Latter-day Saints, I talked with President Kimball one day about sex and sin. He was very concerned about the behavior of youth today and the problems they brought upon themselves being too much of the world.

"What should we teach young women about sex and sin?" I asked President Kimball.

"Tell them, 'Don't do it!' " was his quick reply.

But hold on, there is more! Even if couples don't plan to "go all the way" in sharing sexual affection and intimacy —acting as if they are married when they are not—doing anything like unto it is a sin before God. Did you realize that? You can read about this in the Doctrine and Covenants, section 59, verse 6: "Thou shalt love thy neighbor as thyself. Thou shalt not steal; neither commit adultery, nor kill, *nor do anything like unto it.*" (Italics added.)

Love your neighbor, help that boy next door, but do not play that you are married with him, no matter what!

The Lord has told us "to suffer" (that is, to allow) no unclean ideas even to enter our hearts or heads. They mean trouble. He says, "For it is better that ye should deny yourselves of these things, wherein ye will take up your cross, than that ye should be cast into hell" (3 Nephi 12:30).

In other words, don't even *think* about sinning! You don't even tease or fool around with the sacred issues of God. That is, if you are the kind of quality person you seem to be.

You see, there really isn't a good reason for being disobedient before God. There is no point in getting hurt, suffering a broken heart, a smashed conscience, a physical soiling just because you are crazy over some boy—however appealing he may be.

You may be listening to the wrong voices. Check them out before you act.

You may be ignorant of God's laws—that's why we have included some scriptures in this chapter. But ignorance of the law is no excuse anyplace. Nor does it help you just because you didn't find out the rules before you started playing a dangerous game.

Consider yourself warned and forewarned.

The rules of the Plan of Life require *obedience* or *punishment* for your own good. And there is good reason.

You see, no unclean thing can dwell in our loving, caring Heavenly Father's presence. He wants us back home. He wants us to make it, and someday we all want to do that. Heaven is where joy and fulfillment will come to us. Heaven is perfection. Sin stifles perfection and brings guaranteed pain.

As for today, here on earth, no unclean person—such as one who has had sex out of wedlock, for example—can keep the companionship of the Holy Ghost. Once you lose that precious gift given you at the time of baptism and confirmation, you are in trouble. You no longer have that special, secret, sure guide to what is right and wrong. Then you are in *real trouble.* You'll make all kinds of mistakes that will pile trouble on your back and bring misery to your entire family before you can cry real tears.

Now pay attention to this: It doesn't matter what you are hearing or seeing in the world. God is not a part of the godless. Large portions of television programming, videos, rock concerts, and media include elements damaging to your life today and tomorrow.

What is the answer? What yardstick can you use to measure your actions and choices? How do you know right from wrong? When you were baptized and confirmed you were given the gift of the Holy Ghost. Cultivate that gift. Invite the Holy Ghost into your life. Live purely since the Holy Ghost cannot function in impurity. It is a most precious gift and will tell you right from wrong, instruct you, guide you, and witness to you that you are a child of God, who loves you.

Your own conscience and your inner eternal spirit will caution you, unless you have already sinned, snuffing out this inspiration in your life for the time being. Then you need to ask Heavenly Father's forgiveness in a sincere act of repentance.

The Holy Ghost will teach you the difference between God's way and the way of the world.

It doesn't matter what the kids at school are saying or what darling boys or foolish boys are coaxing you to do for whatever reason (even reasons like "love" or "proof" or "everybody's doing it"). Notwithstanding. Okay?

What does matter is *your life* and *God's will* for you.

These are the true facts.

It is a sin to have sexual intercourse with anyone to whom you are not legally and lawfully married—or anything like unto it!

Some youth get caught, ready or not.

Repentance? Yes. You already have heard about repentance. But maybe what you don't know yet is the pain people suffer when they need to repent. Repenting isn't easy. It is real tough, real emotional. It is a real shameful time of suffering before that cleansing feeling comes and peace and a quiet conscience before God is restored. Spiritual suffering is a worse misery than any physical sickness.

Breaking a habit or giving up a demanding relationship —changing your life—is a most difficult move.

On the other hand, sex (and the hugging and kissing that lead up to it) is a most compelling activity. Be warned. Be aware. Beware!

Some may question how anything so fun, so natural, so accepted, can be a sin? Don't forget, it is a sin only under the wrong conditions. This is so to

—protect the innocent;

—keep procreation on a lofty level; and

—preserve God's purposes in his perfect plan for us.

You see, the first two great sins are murder and adultery (or sex out of wedlock, remember). Think about it this way: both of these actions mock God. Murder is taking life. And that is God's business. Sex is the way life is invited or how babies are created. If this is done under conditions God has not authorized it is a mockery to him. It is taking God's role into your own hands to fool around with life and death—or anything like unto it.

What about birth control? Listen, would you tease somebody by drifting a sharp knife across his throat or playing gun games? No! Though this is not murder, it is pretending . . . and it is frightening. The image carries into sexual activities. Pretending or "anything like unto it," as the scriptures say, is understandably displeasing to God.

Sex is for a wife and her husband. It is the way a couple can develop oneness. It is saved for marriage for the sake of the couple and the children that may come to that couple. It is the ultimate act of intimacy that God has provided to unite a certain special woman with her certain special man so that they come to know each other as they are not known to anybody else. Also, so that they may have the incredible blessing of being earthly parents to others of Heavenly Father's spirit children.

Such a sacred thing as a new spirit's coming from heaven to earth should be surrounded by purity, responsibility, tenderness, maturity, and God's blessings and love. Don't you agree?

After all, it is how *you* were born. And it is how you will want your own precious babies to be born some day.

If . . . if by some sad mistake a baby should come out of wedlock, it is a wise girl who will realize that two wrongs don't make a right. Adoption instead of abortion is the path to consider. Jesus sacrificed his life for us—out of love and understanding of the Father's plan. When such a serious mistake is made as getting pregnant before marriage, the unwed mother should be counseled to consider placing this child in a home established according to God's will where it can grow and develop properly. It is the baby's eternal spirit that belongs to Heavenly Father that must be considered and given every chance.

Children getting married to cover a mistake may not be a right move, either. Great wisdom should be used in dealing with this serious sin, particularly because of the strong emotions attached to such a situation. Parents, bishops and other Church leaders, and professional counselors can offer valuable advice.

In today's world there are too many people who have become so broadminded that it seems their brains are about to fall out. And they want to open all their Christmas presents before the day dawns. It can ruin everything.

So what is left?

Be a bell ringer with boys, but stay out of trouble.

And let see which of you shall bear the bell
To speak of love a-right!

—Geoffrey Chaucer

Be a Bell Ringer
with Boys

You've probably been to a state fair before. So many exciting things to see and do. For generations one of the more popular state fair concessions has been the one where a person can swing a mallet down to a pad, and the force of the blow will send a "birdie" sliding up an enormous scale toward a bell at the top. If the bell rings, the mallet swinger is a bell ringer—a winner—and takes home a prize.

You can be a bell ringer with boys.

You've already learned about bells, belles, and boys. Now let's talk about young women who can make a difference with boys. If boys are so important—and they are in the long scheme of things—it is a wise young woman who values a good relationship with young men.

You can be a young woman who knows how to choose the "better part," as Mary did with Jesus while Martha fretted and fumed and missed the whole point of the Lord's association.

For example, consider this story of Mary Todd and Abraham Lincoln.

When Lincoln was a young man, he had met Mary Todd. There was to be a ball in Springfield, Missouri, where Abe could see this girl. He made preparations to go even though dancing wasn't his favorite thing. He'd been born in a cabin, remember, where social graces had to take a back seat to the hard life of the frontier and nighttime study by candle flame.

The story goes that Lincoln went to the dance and approached Mary. "Miss Todd," he said, "I want to dance with you in the worst way."

They danced, but later Mary confessed to a friend, "He certainly did."

But dancing isn't all there is to life even when you are young. Mary Todd saw something wonderful in Abe, who grew in stature and improved in social skills. He became a beloved president of the United States of America, and she became his wife.

In other words, to be a bell ringer with boys, you need to know more about them than if they "dance in the worst way" and you need to do more for them than dance with them.

Now is the time to learn how to get along with boys—to laugh with them, learn with them, please them, feed them, cheer them, listen to them, heal them, nudge them into righteous behavior, and try to understand them, if you can.

Boys add so much fire to life with their buoyant bravado, their mysterious macho way, their maddening manners, their hello and good-bye style, their unique potentials. It's good to find out early on what you like about boys. What do you respond to or what are you repelled by in a boy? It is good to give thought to such things right now, long before you are to make a lifetime choice or even before you begin real dating.

Remember that boys grow up to be bosses, bishops, professionals, and the repairmen you count on. They become the community leaders, brothers-in-law, as well as husbands and fathers. You will see these boys again— grown-up now and in the fast lane of your life. Today, under low-risk circumstances, you can prepare for that day.

Get to be an expert with boys now; become a bell ringer. Bell ringers are life changers in the sense we are speaking about. A bell ringer, you know, is one who rings an alarm, issues a call, sounds the signal, sets the tone, gets the attention, and makes a difference. That's what you need to do with boys. Let me offer a few suggestions on how to go about that.

Get to know him

When I was a guest in a home one weekend, the teenage daughter returned early from a regional "computer" dance because she and her computer-date partner "weren't having any fun."

That seemed too sad. Young men, young women, dates, dancing, new dress, dream come true! Home early? I began asking questions. What was his name? Where did he live and how long had he lived there? Where was he born? What classes was he taking at school? Did he have a hobby? Were his family converts to Christ? What work did he do after school? How did he get his job? What did he like to do on long summer Saturdays? Was he interested in computers or did he use them just for special dances?

My young friend knew her date's name and school. Period.

They hadn't talked.

She had been with him for a couple of hours and had learned nothing more about this young man than that he hadn't learned to dance very well. Secretly I thought she had fallen down on her end, too, because she hadn't learned to draw him out, to really talk and listen to him, as a girl should be able to do. It's a basic human requirement, or at least opportunity. But this lovely *looking* girl was unprepared for social situations. And she didn't change. To this day it has limited her work and her love life.

Be a friend

Thinking in terms of friendship is a powerful psychological tool for a girl just learning to be a bell ringer with boys. It takes the fear out of dating. It stifles shyness and mental blocks. It opens up a whole new world in relating to boys.

Friendships can be forever—married or not.

When you learn the value in being a good friend, you'll be blessed with many friends. There are a number of interesting, fine, fun, worthy, kind boys around to cultivate. Remember the old saying, "God gave us relatives, but we can make our own friends."

Maybe you've already memorized this poem in school, but in case you think you can't be a bell ringer with boys, just remember these words from William Wordsworth and you'll find your niche:

> Small service is true service while it lasts;
> Of friends, however humble, scorn not one;
> The daisy, by the shadow that it casts,
> Protects the lingering dewdrop from the sun.

Practice conversational skills

Conversation is one way in which you can learn more about one of Heavenly Father's other children.

Think back on the girl who came home early from the dance because they weren't having any fun. Getting to know somebody interesting is fun. Try it, you'll like it.

Your date, for example, could be your town's John Travolta and you could dance all night with your mouth shut and your brain locked. You would go home without knowing much about your partner (or he about you). He'd have no reason to ask you out again and you'd miss an interesting relationship. Besides, he just might be the very boy to tutor you through your computer class!

Develop a talent

The late Elder LeGrand Richards of the Counsel of the Twelve Apostles used to preach to the youth of the Church: "A man can't sit around looking at a pretty face for the rest of his life. Young men, choose a girl who has brains, skills, one who can *do* something!" This is good advice for girls, as well.

The rest of that story is worth hearing, too. Elder Richards preached this philosophy to his missionaries when he was a mission president. Years later as he traveled about the Church as a General Authority, one of his missionaries came up to him after a conference and said, "Elder Richards, I went home from my mission and did what you said. I looked the field of girls over and found one who could do something. She could sing. So I married her. Well, the morning after we were married, I awakened first. I looked over at this girl, her head on the pillow next to mine, and I thought, 'Oh, what have I done?' But then an idea came to me. I gave her a mighty wake-up jab with my elbow and called, 'Wake up and sing. Sing for me! Sing!' "

United States presidents are important people, too. Especially one like Thomas Jefferson. But he wasn't always president—when he was a young man courting his future wife, he nosed out several other suitors. There is a favorite story about this included in *Presidential Anecdotes*, edited by Paul F. Boller, Jr.

One day two gentlemen happened to call on Martha Skelton at the same time. They were friends and decided to go in together. But as they were about to pass from the hall into the drawingroom, they heard some music. Someone was playing the violin, accompanied by the harpsichord, and a lady and gentleman were singing. The visitors knew at once who it must be because Jefferson was the only violinist in the area. The two men then looked resignedly at each other and one said, "We're wasting our time. We might as well go home."

Maybe you can't sing or play an instrument, but you can do your "daisy deed" by becoming the best bell ringing conversationalist of your generation. People of all ages will love you for it. The nice thing about learning to converse is that you can practice on your grandmother, on the children you babysit, on Aunt What's-Her-Name, or on the neighbors.

Do your homework ahead of time. Arm yourself with a long list of questions. Consider ways to gather information after putting him at ease. Share some information about yourself to get things going. Persist. It will pay off.

Stop, look, and listen to him

The most frequently ignored social trait is listening. Asking questions or making comments is only one side of an exchange. Two people talking to each other at the same time about their own interests do not a conversation make. There is no one to listen.

Listening is unselfish. It also can be educational, delightful, and rewarding.

Collisions in coversations can be avoided if you follow your primary school rules for pushing through traffic. Stop. Look. Listen.

Stop and think about what you are going to say. Do it ahead of time so that you are ready when the opportunity comes.

Stop and think about what your partner is saying. Look at his facial expression, his body movements. Does he mean what he says? Is he feeling self-conscious (you see, boys get nervous, too).

Look about you for new ideas to talk about — the rising moon, the couple in front of you, the window display for men's clothing, the new titles in the bookstore, the new building going up, the cheerleader routines from the opposing high school.

Listen with your facial expression, your eyes, and your mind. Listen with your heart as well as your ears so that you can comment and take the exchange another round or two, at least. He won't be able to resist your friendship.

Feed him

Some things never change. Feeding a boy is one of those things. Have a drink of juice or hot chocolate ready when he arrives at your door.

Come up with good food ideas for other occasions. For example, invite him to breakfast on the nearest mountain at sunrise, or brown bag it at the beach for sunset. Take along a feast to pacify tummy growls when you are riding the bus to youth conference. Have pizza ready to pop in the microwave or nacho chips prepared for broiling after the fireside.

When he wins a point or loses the election, leaves for school or a mission, advances in the priesthood, works late, or breaks a leg, get those cookies, muffins, and caramel corn going his way.

You and your girlfriend can prepare your own version of "Babette's Feast" for four. Be as formal and as gourmet as your resources and skills allow. Start young—*now*—and by the time such an endeavor really counts you will be ready.

Be a peacemaker

We're talking about friendship, remember. Bell ringers indicate trends, we said in a previous chapter. If your relationship seems to be ending, maybe you had better do some mending. Swallow your pride and leave the relationship on good terms, even if the two of you will no longer be a romantic item. After all, this lad may grow up to be your bishop!

Some years ago we printed a great poem in the *New Era*. Maybe it will give you some ideas:

Love's Wrath

They quarreled and in cold anger she wrote him:
"I'm returning the letters—the picture—the pin.
I'm also enclosing your valentine (a worthless token).
The lace is all torn—the hearts broken."
With righteous hurt anger he answered the letter:
"I'm returning the tiepin—the gloves—the sweater.
But I'm keeping your kisses (although you regret them).
If you want them returned—please come and get them."
(Alda Brown, *New Era*, March 1971, p. 24.)

Help him

Boys need a lot of help. They like to have a girl interested in them, too. So help him. Without being a nag, a holier-than-thou prude, or a know-it-all bore, your perspective can be invaluable to a boy. For example, if he knows that it is important to a cool girl like you that he be worthy to go on a mission, he is more likely to make those plans. Help him stay worthy to go. Help him understand what a mission can mean to the rest of his life—and to some girl's life, too. Talk to him now about his priesthood assignments.

You know that a deacon collects fast offerings and passes the sacrament. A teacher is a special helper to the bishop and can go home teaching. A priest can baptize as well as prepare and bless the sacrament of the Lord's supper. How does it feel to do these important things? Explain what it means to you and ask him to share his feelings. Compliments about the way he gave the sacrament prayer will strengthen his confidence and your standing in his eyes. Now that is helping!

Be his cheerleader

Everyone needs a cheerleader. It keeps a person from becoming discouraged, feeling unappreciated. It keeps a boy from becoming a tease—and impossible!

A bell ringer is a cheerleader with boys. You are that bell ringer, remember? So you thank him for every little thing he does. Boys do a lot for you, too. They pay your way, carry the heavies, fix your bike, help decorate the gym, letter your campaign poster, support your swim meet, and eat the cookies you baked. So thank them!

Compliment him on being a good worker. Tell him you've noticed (or heard) how dependable he is at work.

Praise him for using clean language. Praise him for not using dirty talk to express himself. Four-letter foul words are unclean and stupid. You are the bell ringer who helps keep this in his mind.

Plan social experiences so that you and your friends can practice what you learn about appropriate behavior in different settings. Then, oh then, be quick to cheer your boyfriend on to great social development. Notice how well he does, even in the smallest way, and compliment him.

Being acceptable *in* the world—though not accepting *of* it, as the scriptures remind us—is important to each disciple of Christ. We are more appealing as we learn and use social skills. We are more confident, and important doors are opened. It simply is more pleasant to be around poised, socially aware boys and girls. And grown-ups! Isn't it now?

A bell ringer is tuned in to etiquette and to what is smart and foolish, gracious or gauche, childish or adult, sinful or civilized.

Be there for him with bells on

If there is anything a boy likes in a girl it is enthusiasm. Show your excitement at seeing him, at being with him. (Hey, no fainting in the halls!)

Laugh at his funnies. (For the hundredth time? Yes!)

Remind him of his great moments with opening statements like, "The game yesterday was great because you . . ." "I will never forget the time you had us all laughing so hard when you . . ." "It was so nice of you to help . . ."

Enthusiasm and a personality with energy can be acquired or learned. Act or pretend you are excited and having a good time, and you will.

Be there for him with bells on, you see. No matter how insecure or ignored or silly you may feel, get busy and make others feel as you'd like to feel. Girls need to be good actresses because they set the mood.

Like mothers. And you will be a mother some day. Mothers rise to the occasion. They are there for all of us with bells on. For example, they know the big presents under the tree aren't for them. They put those presents there themselves. But if they sulked all Christmas day because of that, wouldn't it be dreadful? Instead they act as if that's exactly the way things should be—everybody else getting the big stuff while they get the baby's handprint in clay! And we love mother more than almost anything, don't we?

Being there with bells on is something you can try, learn, and turn into a good habit that brings you much happiness. You'll be a people pleaser.

One last thought. The second great commandment from God is about loving our neighbor as ourself. Love the boys as other children of Heavenly Father. They are important in his kingdom with unique missions to perform.

You can
help,
encourage,
cheer,
understand,
suggest,
nudge,
befriend,
listen to, and
learn from these choice young men.

Get ready. Get psychologically set for enjoying friendly times together. Prepare for these times with energy and friendliness, brightening your smile, sparkling in your eyes, and bubbling over in your chatter.

Now, look at you—a real bell ringing girl!

Give her the bells and let her fly!

—Anonymous

Be a Bell Ringer
with Your Friends

Be a bell ringer with your friends.

Friends are the fun and comfort in life. A friend is someone who likes you no matter what—even in the ragged morning after a slumber party, even if your complexion resembles a poppy seed muffin.

Be a mover, a shaker, an idea girl with plans about how to make a friendship richer and how you and your friend can grow up into pleasant, worthwhile people.

You know about enriched bread, enriched milk—they're good for your body. An enriched friendship is good for your soul; you make it enriched by bringing uplifting thoughts to your discussions. Doing Christian projects together for others and helping each other in self-improvement goals can strengthen your character as well as deepen your relationship. With such a friend you like so much and trust so much, you could think out loud in front of her!

Be a bell ringer as a friend by caring about what you do together. Share brisk ideas for how to spend Sunday. If she isn't a churchgoer, coax her to go with you, like a good friend. She'll probably get so she likes it. Little acts of compassion will draw the two of you closer. Your age group can work happy wonders by visiting shut-ins, lonely single career girls, and heartbroken widows.

Together be good friends to others of your age group. For example, I know two girls about fifteen years old who published a summer news sheet and mailed it to their friends to keep them informed about each other while school was out.

Be a bell ringer as a friend by caring about her!

Remember birthdays by planning small surprises—a bookmark, a cross-stitched "card," a bit of embroidery, a flower, a new hair ribbon for her pigtail or banana curls, or a single cupcake with an enormous candle for a lunch celebration in the school cafeteria.

Remember your friend on her "down days" as well as her birthday. Birthdays only come once a year and down days happen at least every time Dad disciplines, Mom gets mad, brother peaks at her journal, or her hair doesn't turn out right.

Be loyal to your friend and live so that she will have reason to be loyal to you. Guard her secrets well. Be trustworthy.

Be grateful for what your friend does for you. Remember such kindness. Mention it to her.

Keep contention down. As alike as you may be, you still are different. Allow that in each other and enjoy it. Learn from your differences.

Find ways to express your interest in other girls without talking unkindly about them. Gossip comes back to haunt you. Think how you would feel if you were walking in someone else's sandals and were being slandered?

"Neither a borrower nor a lender be," unless you understand what a sticky problem borrowing can be. That has been good advice ever since Shakespeare wrote the phrase nearly four hundred years ago.

Forget about jealousy for any reason. Try, anyway. For example, tell yourself to wait and be patient if it seems someone is taking your friend away. Be patient and still keep loving your friend. She'll be back. Meanwhile, learn more about how to be a friend.

Being a friend and having a heart-to-heart friend means wanting only the best for each other. You are glad for each other's successes and good times. You are sad and share the pain in disappointments. You keep a keen eye on each other's spiritual "condition" and give wise advice about listening to parents and religious leaders.

Some good reading will help you understand the qualities of friendship and character that make for good friends. You'll find wonderful ideas in the Gospels of Matthew, Mark, Luke, and John in the Bible. Read how Jesus treated his friends.

He performed the miracle of the loaves and fishes so that his friends might not go hungry!

He forgave those who were rude to him—even his enemies who sought to take his life.

He taught the Beatitudes as fundamental principles for getting along well with others.

He taught that the way to true friendship is through service. Jesus even washed the dusty feet of his friends.

He taught us to heal others whose needs are great. Our healing may be on a different level from his, but the example is there to teach us to try and make our friends feel better!

Because of what he taught and how he applied these principles in life's situations, Jesus showed all people—even you and me today—how to live, how to bring love into our lives and into the world.

Jesus is a beautiful example of how a friend should think, feel, and act. Jesus is your special friend. He doesn't push in on your life unless you invite him in through prayer. Then he is quick to be comforting, helping, forgiving, lifting, and incredibly loving. He makes you feel good inside your heart, and he is as close as your heart.

One way to be a bell ringer with friends is to establish certain ties with them—ropes or ribbons of experience and thought that bind you together.

When you were a child, you probably heard the story titled *The Little Prince,* by Antoine de Saint Exupery. It is a good one to read again as you try to learn more about how to be a true friend and how to earn a friend who will be true to you.

In this story, the charming little prince came from another planet to visit earth. He enjoyed what he saw but life was lonely. He needed a friend. He wanted to be loved and understood.

He came upon a fox and, after a good morning greeting, the little prince said to the fox, "Come and play with me. . . . I am so unhappy."

"I cannot play with you," the fox said. "I am not tamed."

"Ah! Please excuse me," said the little prince.

But after some thought, he added:

"What does that mean—'tame'?"

"It is an act too often neglected," said the fox. "It means to establish ties."

" 'To establish ties'?"

"Just that," said the fox. "To me, you are still nothing more than a little boy who is just like a hundred thousand other little boys. And I have no need of you. And you, on your part, have no need of me. To you, I am nothing more than a fox like a hundred thousand other foxes. But if you tame me, then we shall need each other. To me, you will be unique in all the world. To you, I shall be unique in all the world. . . . If you tame me it will be as if the sun came to shine on my life. I shall know the sound of a step that will be different from all the others. Other steps send me hurrying back underneath the ground. Yours will call me like music . . . please tame me!"

"I want to, very much," the little prince replied. "But I have not much time. I have friends to discover, and a great many things to understand."

"One only understands the things that one tames," said the fox. "Men have no more time to understand anything. They buy things all ready made at the shops. But there is no shop anywhere where one can buy friendship and so men have no friends any more. If you want a friend, tame me."

You go about "taming" someone into being your friend by finding out about her and about her favorite things. It helps to identify a person's good points, to become acquainted with her family, to see her room and look at her books and treasures.

This, of course, takes time. Friendship doesn't always happen in a hurry, and you can't be *this* interested in everybody. However, you can learn to be a people pleaser. You can naturally be polite and kind though not as involved in the details of another's life as you must if you are building a friendship. Turning a relationship into a real friendship is a lifetime investment of yourself. But it is worth it.

In a good relationship you each give in and give up a little of your personal delights or prejudices, perhaps. You become unselfish! Then you like to do some of the same things. You giggle together. You both might be shocked by some of the stupidities in life. If you like the way you are when you are with her, then your chances are good at having a fine friendship.

Have you read the wonderful little book *The Diary of Anne Frank*? She was a school girl about your age but lived nearly fifty years ago, hiding out in an attic to keep from being killed by the Nazis in those dreadful days for Jewish people. And she kept a diary that has since been published into a book. She wrote, "The reason for my starting a diary . . . is that I have no such real friend. Let me put it more clearly, since no one will believe that a girl of thirteen feels herself quite alone in the world, nor is it so. I have darling parents and a sister of sixteen. I know about thirty people whom one might call friends—I have strings of boyfriends, anxious to catch a glimpse of me. . . . I have relations, aunts and uncles, . . . a good home, no I don't seem to lack anything. But it's the same with all my friends, just fun and joking, nothing more. I can never bring myself to talk of anything outside the common round. We don't seem to be able to get any closer, that is the root of the trouble. Perhaps I lack confidence, but anyway, there it is, a stubborn fact and I don't seem to be able to do anything about it.

"Hence, this diary. In order to enhance in my mind's eye the picture of the friend for whom I have waited so long, I don't want to set down a series of bald facts in a diary like most people do, but I want this diary itself to be my friend, and I shall call my friend Kitty."

Aren't you blessed that you aren't in hiding like Anne Frank? You are free to go forth and find someone with whom you can enjoy a fine friendship at this important time in your life.

You get something very special, something unique from each friend. As you learn to get along closely with one girlfriend, your skills at relating to others will increase. Then your circle of friendship will widen. You can ring bells—or make life more beautiful, you see—for many other friends.

You'll probably learn about Cicero somewhere along the way in school. He was a wise scholar in ancient Greece who wrote the following lines, "What sweetness is left in life, if you take away friendship? Robbing life of friendship is like robbing the world of the sun."

So to make friends, be a bell ringer with people until that certain person-made-for-you becomes friends with you.

Of course, you can be friends with your family, your church leaders, your school teacher, and people your own age from your school or neighborhood. The rules of friendship apply to all human relationships. But in this chapter we're talking about heart-to-heart friends. And that kind of friendship is a gift. It will last only if you take care of it.

Have you ever caught a snowflake and studied it under a microscope for its unique design, comparing it with another and yet another snowflake? Try it sometime. They reveal a miracle of God's creation. Each snowflake is different from the other. So are people. So go ahead and look for a friend who is right for you, not right for someone else or for the most popular girl in school. Find your snowflake, the one who clicks with you, and then "tame" her. Treat her in the most Christlike way you can. Earn her friendship by being a bell ringer, as you've come to understand that meaning.

Oh, never forget how strong peer influence is. You want to be like your friends and you want them to like you. But remember who you are—a daughter of God. Born for a wise and holy purpose, you are a special spirit with a mission on earth to perform. Be sure you choose friends who will be good for you.

You see, it works both ways, doesn't it! You will be influenced and you can influence. A bell ringer is a terrific example and very good influence on her friends.

Be a bell ringer.

The bell never rings of itself;
unless someone swings it, it is dumb.

—Plautus

Be a Bell Ringer
with Your Family

Be a bell ringer with your family. Adam became a bell ringer just by being born.

Adam got his name because he was the firstborn in his family. His father was excited about this new baby he and his wife were expecting. I went to the hospital for the delivery because our daughter-in-law's parents were serving a mission and couldn't be there. A new mother likes support at a time like this!

Our son stood by her side to assist with the miracle of the birthing. I waited just outside of the door. Just seconds after the first sound of the new baby's cry, the door flew open and the proud father burst out to announce to me, "It's a boy. Mom, it's a boy! And I just love him!"

Have you ever seen a brand new, just-born baby? It is *not* the most gorgeous thing in the world. It is a squiggly, squawking, suffering, sticky, red-skinned little creature with matted hair (if there is any hair!). Arms and legs wave and kick, contract and thrust. It is an amazing miniature of humanity.

And our son said he *loved* his newborn.

I knew how he felt—how all parents feel at such a moment. He'd hardly had time to check over his new baby or see it cleaned up from the birth process. He surely hadn't had time to build up any kind of relationship with him, but he loved him already. Awesome! You see, the baby was something—someone—he had helped to create.

"Isn't it wonderful, this loving?" I asked him. Then I went on to say, "Do you know that this is exactly the way I feel about you?"

"It is?" The new father was surprised. His mother loved him the way he loved that new child in there? How could that be? He looked at me somewhat embarrassed because he wasn't feeling for me what he was feeling for his newborn; and here I was, his mother, proclaiming love for him, *my* child.

"Yes, I love you as you love your firstborn. But let me remind you that when Adam is grown and a father, he probably won't feel much different toward you than you do toward me now. My reward is that you love your children as I love you. God loves us more than we love him, too."

We talked for a moment about the miracle of birth and the growth of love. "Though it may be hard to believe at this moment," I said to him, "you will love all your children as much as this one. Our capacity to love our children cannot begin to compare with Heavenly Father's. Now that you have a child, you have a little idea of how Heavenly Father loves you, his spiritual offspring. One day you will learn to love Heavenly Father as your Adam will learn to love you."

You are part of your family by God's assignment. You are his spirit child. He knows where your spirit has been placed—within which family circle—so that you can learn important lessons, develop certain talents, accomplish certain goals, fill a particular mission on earth, and spread your particular sunshine to bless others.

You may have strong parents who bring their children well along the gospel path. You can fit in and follow or you can rebel. It's up to you.

Because of divorce or disagreement in your family you may hear conflicting voices about what is important in life. You can search out truth or go along in confusion. It's up to you.

You may have parents who have not yet received the gospel, who do not understand it, who have not figured out how to live by gospel principles. You will have to fit into this household as your own beliefs dictate.

All over the worldwide Church are marvelous stories of young people who have been baptized and confirmed and are living high standards in homes where parents just don't understand—yet!

You can be a bell ringer by loving your parents anyway and by obeying them as you can. You can help your parents understand the gospel and show them how to live it. You can study and learn all you can about Christ's way of doing things to improve life and prepare people for eternity. After all, that is the purpose of this life—to prepare people for eternity.

A caring parent goes on loving his or her child whether that love is returned or not. The heart expands with boundless love and each additional child is welcomed the same as the first. But, oh, how nice it is, how easy to *like* that offspring as well as love her when she is a bell ringer, a light in the home; a person who makes her house a place of joy and growth; who pitches in with the work, yes, but who also has good ideas for getting along, for growing, for enjoyment, and for being a family of loveable disciples of Christ.

You can be a light of Christ in the home. You can be an example.

You can be a bell ringer!

Make a difference in your family's lives. Learn to be and to do those things that will make your family circle the happiest place on earth for you to be. Then your family can help others do that for other families. It is an exciting possibility.

But first, what is the definition of a family?

Family comes from the Latin *familia*, meaning household (including servants as well as relatives of the householder). *Family* can mean (1) a group of individuals living under one roof and usually under one head, and (2) a group of persons having a common ancestry, a clan.

The Church teaches us that the *ideal* family is the basic unit in society. It consists of a husband and wife who have made covenants before God in a marriage ceremony for time and for all eternity. As the couple has children who are born to them under those covenants or are sealed to them in a holy temple, they become part of this eternal family organization. Then the family strives to help each member live according to God's will. If they succeed they will know peace and joy together now and will qualify for a continued relationship and eternal increase in the next world with Heavenly Father.

Remember, life isn't just for now!

A true eternal family is patriarchal. This means that the father is the head of the family: that is for the purpose of order and peace. You can't have bosses giving conflicting orders and expect peace. In a patriarchal family the father counsels with the mother, for these two are as one, much the way God the Father and Jesus are one, for example. Counseling together is for the good of the family members.

You've learned the definition of *family* from Webster's dictionary and the Church. Now here is my own explanation:

A family is God's way of blessing the world.

A family keeps a mother from doing the things she's always wanted to do until she is too old to do them. But somewhere along the way a family weaves such a magic that one day the mother realizes that this is what she wanted to do all along.

Families are always multiplied by two and come in a wide range of mathematical combinations. This unique variety pack comes in assorted sizes, shapes, colors, dispositions, and bank accounts. Each additional member to the unit challenges, for a time, the lofty premise that all men are created equal—that newcomer gets more attention per hour than everyone else put together. Right? New babies do that.

The youngest member of the circle is termed The Baby. And whether the youngest member is six or sixty, he or she is forever after called The Baby by a loving mother.

Babies cause parents to buy more film, lose more sleep, stay home from more parties for tending duty, and yet babies remind us that heaven is really very close after all.

Yes, babies are for loving.

What about the toddlers?

Toddlers are little destroying angels and may be found wherever there is water. They are also known to slide down the best furniture, sneeze when fed, move restlessly from room to room, leaving their train behind them. The only time they are quiet is when they are doing something they shouldn't. Toddlers have a disarming way of being charming. They smile their sweetest smile when they are about to be disciplined.

Toddlers are for teaching—teaching to sing, to pray, to read, to eat with a fork instead of fingers, to understand that training pants are the road to freedom, to know right from wrong, and to recognize the difference between Jesus and Santa Claus. One of the nicest things about a toddler is that he or she loves you unabashedly.

Oh, toddlers are for loving.

Grade-schoolers around the house are part of the family, too. They are famous for giggles and gum, for the blank spaces in the front of their smiles, for freckles and telling family secrets to the neighbors.

They are famous for running—running noses, running away, running errands, and for running the bathroom water the longest with the least to show for it.

They are for getting—getting measles at Christmas and into trouble when you aren't looking. They are good at getting things into drawers already too full, and things out of closets that shouldn't have been opened in the first place. They ask more questions and eat more times a day than anybody had in mind.

Grade-schoolers are great at losing—losing sweaters, ski caps, one glove, boots, balls, books, lunch pails, and instructions. They are devoted to creatures of the earth that growl, slither, wiggle, or crawl. Grade-schoolers collect things that creep and crawl, and slink, growl and make a mess—and things like rocks, wrappers, bottles, cans, elastics, and baseball cards. They have a big fan club made up of proud parents and grandparents, of teachers and big sisters, especially when they perform in the school program.

Oh, grade-schoolers are for loving.

Teenagers in the family grow too much too soon, or too little too late. They make our hearts warm with their young beauty of body, their quickness of wit, their fierce loyalties and the fact that they surprise us on occasion with an extravagant gift.

Teenagers are challenges and they are challengers. They challenge authority, decisions, life-style, the system, adults' taste in music, and anybody's turn to have the car. They are smarter, stronger, and more spiritual than their responsible elders who begged, lifted, dragged, fought, paid, and loved them to where these teenagers are today.

Families are for loving each other anyway because, you see, families are God's way of blessing the world. Oh, thank God, families are forever!

And you, as the chief catalyst in the family (because you are your kind of girl) can help your family be a bell ringing family. You can love each person. You can look to making them happy instead of growling about your own problems.

Oh, help God bless the world with good families. Be a bell ringer with your own family and watch the magic spread from house to house.

Actually, you were born to be a bell ringer, but now that you've grown considerably it's time to take a look at how you can ring those bells and shake up good situations for your family at this stage of life.

To be a bell ringer with your family suggests that you will do those things that will help your family become an ideal family so that all the tomorrows through all eternity you can enjoy each other's companionship. You will want to be together because you will like each other as friends as well as love each other as relatives.

*Like sweet bells jangled,
out of tune and harsh.*

—William Shakespeare

CHAPTER

Be a Bell Ringer in Public

There was a sturdy football player who wanted to go over big with girls, so he asked his cool big brother what he should do. The brother said, "Give a girl compliments and you can't lose. Everyone likes to be complimented."

That night at the dance the younger brother was struggling with his overweight partner. He tried and tried to think of a compliment he could give her to ease the stress of the situation. He finally thought of something.

"Say, for a fat girl, you certainly don't sweat much!"

What do you think about what he said?

Two girls were eating frozen yogurt at a sidewalk table. One was licking her treat with noisy slurps and smacks. Suddenly she stopped, stared off into space, and said to her friend, "You know, the telephone is driving me crazy. It never rings for me!"

Can you think of maybe one reason why?

At the basketball game the young man turned to his date and said, "Watch that player over there. Before the season is over he'll be our best man."

With her eyes glowing the young woman said, "Oh, honey! What an unusual way to propose marriage!"

Some people mean well, but they manage to make the social blunders anyway. You know better than that though. You are a real bell ringer in public. Well, aren't you? In case there is a question, here are some things to think about.

To be a bell ringer in public places, at school, work, and church, requires further personal preparation. You need to know what is acceptable to grown-ups, to bosses, to religious leaders, and to the principal.

Your own age group feels more at ease around someone who knows what to do when. For instance, today's social bell ringer is the girl or boy who is calm but caring when the punch is spilled, who doesn't stammer during introductions, who has confidence and poise around newcomers and grown-ups.

People of all ages enjoy that secure, relaxed feeling which surrounds the young woman who comes equipped with social know-how.

Social success is important. It opens doors for greater opportunity. It helps you beat your competitors *off* the athletic field. It helps you to be pleasing to others. It makes life more pleasing, too.

Look at it this way, if you are going fishing and you want to catch fish, you take fish bait—worms and flies. You surely won't bait the hook with your own favorite food (fudge, strawberries, or whatever). You take the food that is favorite with fish. So it is with social behavior. You do what will make others feel comfortable.

The whys and whatsits of etiquette can be confusing and frustrating, though, if you let them. On the other hand they can be the buffer between you and your public. They are the semaphores in social traffic.

Good manners do matter!

It is foolish to toss aside the matter of manners simply because the details seem too involved. Behind every rule is the basic philosophy of treating other people exactly as you'd like to be treated yourself. Keep this ancient success secret always in mind, and then study up on etiquette rules themselves. All of this can determine how successful you'll be in your public appearances as well as your relationships with your boss, the public you serve through working after class, the teachers and leaders at church and at school, and when you participate at social events.

Good manners are not an affectation. They are an outward expression of our inner feelings toward others. They don't cover up for lack of character, either; they reflect the fact of it.

At church

Appropriate behavior includes speaking with a softer voice, walking with a slower step, keeping your hands to yourself, and speaking to others to show that you believe we all are brothers and sisters in Heavenly Father's family.

Your appearance should reflect how you would want to look if you were to meet Christ. After all, you are in the house of the Lord, so look like it. Save the Halloween look for another time, if you are into trendy fashions. More modest hair and clothing styles are best, and be certain that the grooming of your hair and body in back is as attractive and immaculate as in front. People sitting behind you will appreciate your concern.

Chewing gum and eating treats is for babies and toddlers. Combing hair, clipping nails, and personal grooming is for your own room at home. Appraisal of your molars should be left for the dentist's chair.

When it's your turn to pray, use the language of prayer. When it's your turn to be silent, be silent and attentive during the prayer. Close your eyes and bow your head out of respect for God. Listen! Then join in an audible "Amen" at the end.

At work

Dress as if you mean business—not pleasure.

Work as if your career depended upon it. It does.

Work as if you want to have the job tomorrow. You need it!

Work to learn.

Work to serve.

Work to earn.

Work to go to bed unashamed and satisfied.

And encourage your many, adoring boyfriends to stay away during your working hours.

Be a bell ringer at work. Some of this may seem troublesome, like ancient history behavior, or boring. But you are somebody special and so you'll want to look and act accordingly. Take it from this grown-up, the working place is no place to look and act like an ordinary teenager. Yes, there are many sick or confused people out there who have given up on the nice things in life. They're the noise makers, the attention getters, and are not very smart at that. But there are many, many choice and charming people who understand the value of self-control and being socially appropriate.

At play

When you are among other people—at church, school, work, or play—there are situations requiring your best social skills. Let's talk about introductions, for example.

Instead of memorizing rules about introducing one person to another, memorize feelings. This is one of the situations for using gospel principles in the social world.

Say the name first of the person you want to honor. Honor your father and mother by saying their names first, then the names of your friends. If it is the principal of the school, maybe you'll feel more respectful saying his name first and then the names of your parents.

Honor the special guest, the General Authority, the important person there by saying his or her name first. Then indicate others by giving their names.

It is helpful and thoughtful to add an item of interest about those being introduced to each other. It gives them something to talk about to each other.

Now, when you are being introduced to someone, concentrate. Listen to the name. Take note of her credentials. When you respond to the introduction, be sure and repeat her name as it was given to you. And smile, looking that person right in the eyes. Even if you think you will faint! Offer a firm handshake instead of a wet sponge or an arm pump.

Social skills aren't something one is born with, like a gift for singing. They must be learned and practiced anew by each generation and modified only as need and changing customs dictate. Treating each other graciously, eating with refinement, and behaving with propriety in public are marks of a caring child of God and certainly improve the life-style of any intelligent person.

On the phone

Always give your full name to identify yourself when making a phone call unless you are absolutely positive the person you are calling knows you by a partial name and knows your voice as well. This saves on confusion and embarrassment of mistaken identity.

Answering the phone is an important behavioral skill at anyone's home or office. Your best voice, your friendliest tone, your most helpful attitude should be used. Telephone calls are impromptu, so prepare the person on the other end of the line if you want to engage them in a long conversation. It is also a kindness to someone who calls you to let them know of any pressure you may be under at the moment. There may be a more convenient time for him or her to call you.

Evening out

Boys invite girls. Boys pay the bills. Girls wait—for the invitation and while the boys pay. Girls also are very appreciative. It is costly to dine out these days. So girls, be excited and verbal about your gratitude. A boy assists a girl with her coat, her chair, and down difficult trails (like a dark theater aisle, a cluttered cafe path, across a busy intersection).

In return a girl gives the boy every opportunity to treat her like a lady. He neither expects nor demands, and she neither succumbs nor initiates a display of affection for an evening out together. Each has the responsibility to make things pleasant, stimulating, and memorable, but it is really up to the girl to set the fun tone of the evening.

An evening out can be informal; it can be casual; but it should not be careless.

How to say NO!

"Thanks just the same, but, no thanks!"

That is a phrase often easier read than said—depending, of course, on the taunts of the crowd and the strength of your willpower in a moment of temptation.

Whether it is an invitation to take a beer "just this once," or to park and pet on Lonely Lane, or to break the Sabbath day, a girl is wise who knows how to say no gracefully and make it stick.

The sooner you master this social skill, the better you can use it. In today's world you need this.

Saying no in any other language may be just as meaningful, but learning to say it in more words than one is a trick you would do well to master. A wise phrase lightly spoken can ease the tension of crowd teasing. A ready answer can stall further temptation. A bit of wit can shift the mood. And your point will have been gained without insult or offense.

A holier-than-thou approach not only is unbecoming and uncalled for but usually adds fuel to a crackling blaze —it makes the group more determined than ever to break down smug defenses.

You don't want that to happen. Your basic reasons for refusal should be well grounded. You should know *why* you don't want to smoke, drink, park, go slumming, do drugs, cheat, or steal.

Your refusal should be based on a firm personal conviction arrived at by study, an understanding of gospel principles and gospel behavior, observance of the lives of others, and prayer for guidance.

In other words, don't lean your case on "my mother says I can't" or "my Church says no."

Know for yourself, answer for yourself, and the results will be far better. Don't listen to the foolish suggestion that everyone is doing it. The fact is that not everyone is doing it. No one with good sense is.

A mannerly person

A mannerly person is careful. Wet weather requires its own cautions. If you are a guest and your coat is wet, turn it inside out before placing it someplace where it won't cause soil or damage. Leave your boots outside unless you are invited to bring them in. If you don't wear rain gear on your feet in stormy weather, remove your shoes to save the flooring. Or be sure that they are thoroughly dry and clean.

When using sporting equipment belonging to someone else, treat it even better than you would your own. If you spoil or break something, you are obligated to pay to replace or repair it. If the owner sincerely refuses your offer, then see to it that you send a gift of some kind or do a kind favor for them.

If a member of your friend's family dies or is seriously ill, you'll want to express concern and friendship. A note, a small gift, some food specialty from your house is a warm way of saying that you are sorry, sad, and concerned.

Anyone who pitches in to put up or take down chairs, tables, decorations, banners, posters, scenery, or signs without having to be asked is special. When it's your turn to be chairman of something, you'll understand just how great it is to have mannerly, helpful you on the scene.

No wonder you are a bell ringer in public.

If you love not the noise of bells,
why do you pull the ropes?

—Thomas Fuller

Ring Those Bells

A young woman and I sat together on the side of Shepherd's Hill in Jerusalem looking across a shallow gully to Bethlehem. As we watched the sun set behind that sacred town, we were suddenly conscious of a special sound—the jingle jangle from several bells strapped around the neck of a ram leading a flock of sheep and goats right in front of us. The animals were moving from their daytime grazing field to their nighttime place next to a primitive tent home of the shepherd which we could see off to the right.

Dutifully the sheep followed their leader with his copper and brass bells sounding the way.

"Suddenly it is Christmas in Bethlehem," exclaimed the young girl beside me. And I agreed.

It wasn't really the season of Christmas, but because of the bells in that particular place, of course we were reminded of the joyful feelings that come with the celebration of Christ's birth.

A small girl—oh, smaller than you—dressed up in her Halloween costume as a Salvation Army Santa Claus, complete with the relentless tingle-tingle of a bell on a long black handle, and went her way for treats. Her bag was full when she knocked at one last door. The lady of the house said she was sorry but her store of goodies was empty— every last treat had been handed out.

The young Santa began ringing her bell merrily and said, "That's okay. I have plenty. I'll give you some of mine!"

It has indeed been said, "A little child shall lead them." What a bell ringer that little girl was.

A time ago in Europe, I was touring with fifteen American teenagers—fourteen girls and one boy—and decided to stop in a roadside retreat in Germany. It was Saturday evening and we had been sightseeing all afternoon. We welcomed the comfort of the little park to wait for the tour bus. The shade of the trees and the water bubbling over ancient sculpture in a small fountain were cooling and soothing. We were weary and sat in rare silence.

And then we heard bells, first one mighty clang from a bell tower in a nearby church. Then the echo seemed to touch off all the bells in all the steeples of the city. It was a thrilling time. There were long moments with hundreds of bells ringing with different tones, not in any harmony or rhythm but each of the bells merrily ringing on its own speed according to its own echo chamber. We wondered at this occurrence. We surely never heard anything like this in America. There just aren't that many bells in any community. Was war being declared? A wedding? A town crisis? Was some festival beginning? Any of these things could be true, for the town bells announced many moods. We later learned that these were vesper bells, signaling the twilight time preceding the Sabbath day. We were full of wonder and warmth at such a time and such a marvelous sound sent off to remind us to prepare for the following sacred day.

When Brigham Young's home, the Beehive House, was being restored in the late 1960s in Salt Lake City, the committee was using the diary of a teenage daughter of Brigham Young as their "guide" book. She was living at the house at the time of her entries. She wrote of paint and wallpaper, room sizes, details of who slept where and what accessories were used to decorate various rooms.

She also spoke of a doorbell. One of the architects on the restoration committee scoffed at that idea. Obviously this young woman's journal entries about the Beehive House could not be taken seriously. Doorbell, indeed! There was no electricity in those pioneer days.

The house had been extensively remodeled for various uses over the many years since this little girl lived there. When the restoration got fully underway, a string pull by the front door was uncovered. Amazing! The string cord went along the ceilings of the halls and parlors to the kitchen area where a small, sharp-toned bell was attached. When someone pulled the cord by the front door it set the clapper jingling against the small bell in the kitchen. Behold! A doorbell. Visitors at the main gate were announced.

Her journal entries with their descriptions about the Beehive House were taken more seriously after that.

A recent girls' camp near historic Nauvoo, and on a separate occasion a Boy Scout jamboree in the same setting, were especially exciting events for me. Everything was worked out to perfection. Because these were both wilderness camps of a sort, effective communication was important. An enormous bell was struck to announce prayer time, wake up, lights out, emergency, and camp congregations of various kinds.

When the gong sounded for dinner, it got the response of every camper. One young woman about your age turned to me at the sound of the gong and said, "Saved by that bell! It is the sweetest sound on earth, heralding my favorite camp activity—chow time."

When Camilla Kimball, wife of President Spencer W. Kimball, was about your age, she kept a journal. She has gone from the earth now, but reading her journal makes it easy to see why she became the partner to a prophet. She was always a bell ringer.

In her journal entries she wrote about the terrible conditions that the Mormon colonists were forced to live with under the Mexican rebels. Later she drew on those journals to compose a life story edited by her son Edward Kimball: "By 1911 the rebels demanded horses, saddles, and food from the colonists, paying with worthless receipts, and they stole anything they could get their hands on. Father lost dozens of head of cattle and horses. We lived in dread. . . .

"[One] evening father came home with word that . . . we should leave for El Paso immediately. . . . We were allowed to take just one trunk of clothes for Father's family of thirteen. I wanted so much to put in my doll and some other treasures, but there was no room. . . ."

They traveled all day and night at a snail's pace and in uncomfortable circumstances, always worried about the threatening rebels who wanted to waylay them. The entry continues:

"Finally, just as dawn was breaking, we crawled slowly across the Rio Grande and were greeted by the sight of the Stars and Stripes. A great shout went up from all [of us] refugees. That sight brought a thrill that is revived in me every time I return to the United States and see the flag again.

"The kind people of El Paso met us at the depot and took us in automobiles (only the second time I'd ridden in one) out to a big lumberyard, where they improvised shelter for the refugees. . . . They put us into a huge corral with dust a foot deep, flies swarming, noisy, stinking, and crowded with a mass of humanity. It was enough to make the stoutest heart sink. . . .

"We felt humiliated as newspaper photographers and reporters recorded our pitiful dependence and as the curious townspeople gawked and pointed at us, as they would animals at a zoo. . . .

"My feeling is that each of us has the potential for special accomplishment in some field. . . . We should all be resourceful and ambitious, expanding our interest. Forget self-pity, and look for mountains to climb."

Sister Camilla was a bell ringer.

When a young woman named Sarah was twelve, her story was reported in the *Church News* and they labeled her Miss Sunshine. But I'd call her Miss Bell Ringer.

Sarah learned about a man in Texas suffering incredibly and homebound with complications from an eczema-like disease. But now his days are brighter. Sarah has written this man much older than she is and she has sent him cards, drawn him pictures, flooded him with small surprises by mail for the purpose of brightening his life some. It has worked. Lance Brunson knows that in all the world he is not alone. Sarah Ferguson cares!

When Jill Hayes celebrated a special birthday, her parents had a big party and invited certain people to pay a small tribute to their talented daughter who had survived early open heart surgery while she was a cheerleader in high school. One of the speakers brought six different kinds of bells: cow bells, oriental bells, wedding bells, miniature bells, hand-painted porcelain bells, and silver Christmas bells. She held up each bell and used it to describe a fine quality Jill was known for. The bells were then presented to Jill as collectables and the beginning of a new hobby for this beloved young woman.

A bell marked the beginning of the Young Women's organization, a move to retrench from the world that is applicable today.

Perhaps those incidents will tell you why bells are a beautiful symbol for your life.

Bells, you recall, have historically been used to give the time of day, to warn of danger, to highlight a celebration, to announce a birth or death, to predict victory or toll defeat, to signal that church is to begin or recess end, that a miracle has happened or someone needs help.

A bell ringer, we learned in chapter 2 of this book, is also called the tintinnabulator! This is the one who pulls the cord to sound the bell. It is the bell ringer, according to source books, who does the ringing. A bell isn't a bell until it is rung! So the bell ringer has special powers and has always been highly regarded.

As you are!

Be a good bell ringer. That's what this book is all about.

Warn, announce, signal, call together, celebrate, indicate trends, and do it in your own special, inimitable, important way.

Good bell ringers—beautiful and strong examples—are needed in today's world. And you are one.

Be a bell ringer for your girlfriends and boyfriends; for your family and for people in your public world of school, work, and church; for your neighborhood and talent training sessions.

Be a bell ringer for God.

Learn and teach. Pray and testify to others at appropriate times and places. Live and help others (boyfriends, parents) to be worthy of filling missions some day. Retrench from the world in an exemplary way as Brigham Young and other prophets today have reminded us.

Be a bell ringer with those who aren't as blessed as you are to know what you know about the plan of life and how people on earth are supposed to live so they can make it home to heaven again.

Now, be a bell ringer about your own life.

Blinde fortune did so happily contrive,
That we as sound as bells did safe arrive.

—Jeremy Taylor

CHAPTER

Questions and Some Answers

Cathy put the last sandwich into one of the brown bags lined up on the kitchen counter. Eight lunch sacks ready to go with her brothers and sister after they had snatched breakfast before heading for the school bus stop. She'd worked on those lunches nearly an hour and it still wasn't quite light outside yet.

She'd already labeled each bag with a name. Sandra didn't like tuna. Jason got sick on peanut butter, while Ben would eat only peanut butter sandwiches. Matt pulled his bread apart first thing to see if there was even a trace of butter or margarine. He was into fitness—fat was a no no. Turkey breast with a thick wedge of lettuce was his lunch order! Eight different lunches. Those sacks had to have names on them or she'd hear about it at dinner if someone got the wrong sandwich.

Cathy yawned as she folded down the top of each bag. She'd been up forever, it seemed, in a house so quiet she shivered from more than cold. It was the hardest part of the day for her every day. Everybody else snoozed away while she played Miss Cinderella.

Today was worse than usual because it was her birthday, too. No one would remember. Sixteen and she'd grown old before her time. Suddenly Cathy was bone tired and tears began to streak her cheek. She dropped to the kitchen stool and laid her head down on her folded arms resting on the countertop. She gave in to self-pity and let the sobs come. No one to hear. No one to care.

It wasn't just lunches; it was dinner, laundry, helping the little kids with homework and practicing their instruments, keeping track of their stuff, and prodding about projects. It was bedtime baths. It was last-minute mending and finding and settling arguments. It was juggling schedules for soccer and Cub Scouts, music lessons and neighborhood birthday parties. It was grocery shopping and food preparation. It was monstrous.

And besides all of the household chores, she was chief comforter to the whole bunch of them, one way or another, but there was no one to comfort her!

Cathy cried all the tears she'd held back ever since Mom's funeral long months ago. She wanted to be brave in front of the younger kids. She'd promised Dad. But this morning a dark cloud of disappointment at the way life had gone plus a deep loneliness filled her whole being. Where was Mom? Who needed her in heaven more than they needed her on earth? What kind of God would work things this way? She mumbled a kind of prayer in her heart to a God she was sure had forgotten her.

"I'm only sixteen—today! Sixteen! Happy birthday to you, Cathy. Ha! Well, I can't do all this. I don't want to do all this. I'm trying but I need someone to help me, too.

Heavenly Father, I need someone to care about me, too."
She rested there a moment, spent from her tears of frustration, sadness, and self-pity.

Then she became aware of a warming in her heart. Suddenly she felt as if she had arms enveloping her, holding her, filling her with comfort and love.

She lifted her head and opened her eyes to look around. No one was there. Still the feeling didn't go but grew stronger as Cathy gave in to a marvelous moment. It was a gift from heaven. It was an answer to prayer. It was proof that God lived and loved her. It was enough.

Keep Cathy's story in mind as you read the following questions and answers. Cathy's mother died and circumstances forced her into a role she didn't expect so soon in life. She needed to know God's love to carry on.

Your circumstances may be different, but you need to know that the Lord loves you, too. Maybe you live in a difficult situation. Maybe you are dealing with a quarreling family, placing your illegitimate child for adoption, worrying about dangerous substance abuse by a family member, or suffering personal illness instead of enjoying youthful good health. The point is, if you *know* the gospel, you can live it and use it for solving life's problems.

Perhaps these questions and answers will be helpful to you.

Q. You have talked a lot about keeping a strong, close relationship with the Lord. Why is it important to do this? And how do I do it?

A. It is important to keep a strong, close relationship with the Lord because he is your Savior. He died so that you might live eternally. He shows you how and helps you do those things that will take you home to heaven again.

He is your example and friend. He'll see you through each day, if you will let him.

He will comfort you when others can't or don't!

But he doesn't force himself on you. Jesus waits so you can *choose* to have him part of your life.

Never forget, whether you turn to Jesus or not, he goes on loving you, waiting for you to love him back.

Some of the ways you can develop and keep a strong relationship with the Lord include:

1. *Studying the scriptures.* As you read the scriptures, more truth will come more easily until at last you understand better what God has to say to you about yourself and this life.

2. *Obeying his word.* When you obey his commandments and do his will, you feel more peace. Your conscience is clear. Doing what is right is proof of your love for him.

3. *Being thankful.* When you count your blessings from God, you will feel a swelling of gratitude within you and you will know the Lord loves you.

4. *Praying.* When you pray you can draw close to God and he will draw close to you.

There is a great scripture that you could work in counted cross-stitch for your bedroom so that you would see it everyday: "Learn of me, and listen to my words; walk in the meekness of my Spirit, and you shall have peace in me" (Doctrine and Covenants 19:23).

Peace! That means happiness or contentment no matter what is going on in your life. This is another important reason for keeping close to the Lord and praying.

Q. Prayer is something else you have suggested to help make life easier. I am fourteen now and I have said my prayers each night at bedtime for as long as I can remember. Until lately, that is. Sometimes—now that I am grown-up—I feel self-conscious or silly doing that. So I don't do the personal prayer thing much anymore.

A. It is important to pray. The Lord has told us to pray to Heavenly Father in *his* name, that is, in the name of Jesus Christ.

This is the way you communicate with your Heavenly Father. You don't have face-to-face conversations with God. At least not yet. You don't use the phone, and you don't send Fax or computer copies from your house to a heavenly mansion. Your eternal spirit (the part of you that lasts forever even after the body is placed in a grave) is the offspring of Heavenly Father. He loves you. (Read Chapter 3 again!) He is interested in how you are doing. Prayer is your way to talk it over with him.

He is interested in what you need.

He is interested in how you are responding to temptation.

He is interested in whether you are conscious that he is the giver of all the good things in life. Do you count blessings, for example?

He is interested in what is breaking your heart.

He is interested in your goals, values, and struggles toward self-improvement.

He is particularly interested in how you are progressing in the gospel. What *do* you know about the kind of life you should be living? The things you do and think will determine whether you can make it back into a loving God's presence some day—that is, whether you will get "home" again.

Q. What is Christ to me? I guess I know the prophet is important to him but what about me?

A. Jesus Christ is your example and friend. He will see you through each day, if you will let him. He is interested in whether you are keeping spiritually alert and morally and physically clean so that the gifts of the Holy Ghost can be yours. It is through the Holy Ghost and counting all the blessings that God has given you already that confirms to your soul that he loves you.

Q. How do I begin to draw close to Jesus?

A. Start now to renew your childhood habit of kneeling down each night before bed in holy communion with Heavenly Father.

Since you claim to be a grown-up now, you are no doubt ready for morning prayers as well as bedtime prayers. Morning prayers are a time to ask for blessings to protect you and help you do what is right all day so that you may have his Spirit with you. Morning prayers are often of gratitude for watching over you while you were sleeping, "out of it" and vulnerable. In your morning prayers you'll pray over tests you'll take at school, a crisis that you have to deal with, and the strength to resist temptation. You may even pray for a needed nudge to do Christlike deeds for others. Bad habits and weaknesses are more easily overcome if you pray for help. With God nothing is impossible, you know.

The more you communicate with God, the more you pray, the less self-conscious you will feel. Prayer, it says in a beloved hymn, is the soul's sincere desire. Prayer can change a dark night of the spirit into a sunny spring day kind of feeling. Try it and you'll see!

Q. Tell me, do grown-ups really kneel down and pray?

A. Yes. Grown-ups really do kneel down and pray to God. All the time. They pray in a lot of places in addition to their bedsides. They pray in their offices and over their cash register totals. They pray over their flocks and their fields because God has told them to and has promised that if they ask in faith for his help it shall be given to them. They pray in a quiet classroom before the students come charging in. They pray over their children and loved ones all the time. They pray for greater understanding of you!

They pray that they may be helpful to you. I am an adult and I know this to be so.

Adults pray over their Church callings constantly. They really want to help you and other children of our Heavenly Father.

You can do this, too. He will hear your prayers. You will feel this.

I remember talking to some missionaries about what they had learned since they had gone into the mission field. One bright and sensitive Elder replied, "I've learned that praying without preparation is like going tracting without your shoes on. You don't get very far. So I have learned to stay on my knees until I feel different."

Good point.

Q. We sing the song "I Am a Child of God," but how can I *know* that this is true and that God is there for me?

A. Try praying and see. I promise you that you will know that he is there for you. We sing that song a great deal because it is a kind of testimony about a wonderful secret that is ours—we are God's spirit children, and what's more, he *loves* us. Loves *us!*

Here are two scriptures for you to memorize and take comfort in.

"For in him we live, and move, and have our being . . . , For we are also his offspring" (Acts 17:28).

"For the Spirit itself beareth witness with our spirit, that we are the children of God: and if children, then heirs; heirs of God, and joint-heirs with Christ" (Romans 8:16–17).

Q. I am a new member of the Church. I am anxious to learn what everything means. There are a lot of phrases and words that I am unfamiliar with, such as *Saint* and *General Authority*, and *recommend*. Help!

A. For your help we are including a brief glossary of some terms, an explanation of some expressions, some definitions of words and phrases and traditions that are familiar to long-time members of the Church but may be new to you.

Saint: The Apostle Paul wrote to members of the Church addressing them as "Saints." We use the word with the same loving meaning today—people who are disciples of Christ, who are among God's chosen people to do his work on earth, who try to live close to God's commandments.

General conference: A gathering of LDS Church members in the historic Salt Lake Tabernacle on Temple Square in April and October. Meetings are held under the direction of the First Presidency of the Church, and the speakers include General Authorities, with music by the Tabernacle Choir and other special choirs as invited. This two-day conference is for the sustaining of General Authorities and general officers of the Church, for financial and statistical reports, and for the uplifting of the Saints. The sessions are broadcast far and wide by satellite.

Some training sessions are held in connection with these semiannual events. Priesthood leadership fill the center section of the Tabernacle. It is very thrilling to witness this brotherhood from many nationalities.

There is special audio equipment available for visitors from non-English–speaking nations to hear a translation of the proceedings in their own language. The translators sit in booths in the basement of the Tabernacle.

Fast meeting: This is not necessarily the opposite of a long meeting! Fast meeting is held once a month, usually on the first Sunday. Members fast two meals on this day. They are served the sacrament as part of the fast meeting. Babies can be named and given a father's blessing. Those who have been newly baptized may be confirmed in this meeting, too. The rest of the meeting is turned over to the spontaneous response from members of the congregation as they are moved upon by the Holy Ghost to stand and bear witness that they know that Jesus is the Christ and that the gospel is true. Other expressions of gratitude and testimony are often shared. A contribution to the poor is made in a "fast offering" to the ward bishop in the amount of the meals the family or individual has missed as part of the fast. Tithes and other offerings are often turned into the bishop on this day, too.

Deseret: A Book of Mormon term meaning "a honey bee" (see Ether 2:3). It became well used by the early settlers in Brigham Young's time to describe Mormons. Deseret is synonymous with ambition, thrift, industriousness, and cooperation. When Utah was a territory, the people called this place the state of Deseret and the beehive later became the symbol of the state of Utah.

Recommend: A recommend is given by the bishop or branch president to a member of the Church in good standing who has been interviewed as to personal worthiness and who is desirous of participating in sacred Church ordinances, such as getting a patriarchal blessing, being baptized for the dead, or getting married in the temple.

Patriarchal blessing: Patriarch means "father," so this is a special blessing from Heavenly Father given by an ordained patriarch to one who has presented a recommend for this choice experience and who is seeking this special guidance from God. The blessing also reveals one's lineage in the house of Israel. This blessing is usually given only once. A record of this blessing is kept at general Church headquarters.

Temple marriage: A sacred ceremony performed in one of the LDS temples dotting the world and performed by one having authority to unite a couple for time and for all eternity. They are promised awesome blessings that are dependent upon their faithfulness to God's commandments. The couple each need a bishop's recommend to participate in this new and everlasting covenant.

Temple sealing: An ordinance performed for couples who have been legally married and who have prepared themselves to qualify for an eternal marriage. Usually they must prove themselves for at least a year after a civil or legal ceremony before coming to the temple. Their children can also be sealed to them at this time.

Baptism for the dead: In a special baptism ceremony, a living person is proxy or stands in for a person who has died without being baptized. Baptism by immersion is necessary for all people to enter into the presence of God. This is according to the mind, the will, and the word of God. Doing baptisms for the dead in one of the temples of God is a favorite activity of sacred service among Latter-day Saint youth.

Q. My relationship with my parents has changed completely since I became a teenager. I can't talk to them about things that are so important to me. I'm in a panic. What can I do?

A. Calm down! It's normal. Maybe that is the first thing you should remember. They haven't changed. You have. If you think you have trouble getting used to this new situation, you should be a parent looking at what has happened to their darling little child who was excited because she forgot to leave a carrot for the Easter Bunny! You are not only a stranger to them, you often are a shock. You know more than your parents do *about some things.*

You have your own friends, your own work schedule, your own money, and maybe even your own car. But unless you are eighteen in the United States, you do not have a legal entity yet. You are still responsible to your parents and they for you before the law. And they always must answer to some degree for you before God. Because families can be forever it is even more imperative that you learn to get along and find love in these new conditions. Cultivate your parents as you would a new friend, and they will want to do the same for you. Stay calm. Be patient. Be prayerful together. Keep going to church together and studying the scriptures together. The Lord will bless you. You'll both be grateful for this new relationship that will last through your adult years.

It says in the Bible that "one generation shall praise thy works to another, and shall declare thy mighty acts" (Psalm 145:4). Since you and your parents don't like the same music, food, or clothing, usually, you might begin your new relationship as friends by speaking of the Lord. That is what this Psalm counsels!

Q. How do we know prayers are answered?

A. You know that prayers are answered by the evidence. Sometimes we don't get *our* way in how we'd like them answered, but always our prayers are heard; if not at once, then finally, we see this. The Lord gives us what is best for us at the time. It is for us to ask him for help, blessings, and guidance.

Here is a delightful story about bells and about answers to prayers.

Some years ago there had been a drought in the great Salt Lake Valley. President David O. McKay was conscious of this hardship on the people. The farmers were in serious trouble because their livestock and the harvest were threatened by lack of water.

One day President McKay was to dedicate the new carillon or bell tower that had been placed on Temple Square in Salt Lake City to hold the historic Nauvoo bell.

In his dedicatory prayer, President McKay fervently asked Heavenly Father for an end to the drought and for blessed moisture that would soften the soil, nourish the grain and crops, and provide water for the livestock.

Across the street to the east there was a huge excavation site that was to become a three-level parking lot beneath the new high rise Church office building. Work was moving along according to schedule at that site—that is until the day of the dedication of the bell tower.

President McKay prayed for rain.

And the rains came!

And came. And came. The crops were moistened and the thirst of the cattle was quenched by the healing rains.

But something else happened.

The parking terrace excavation across the street filled with water!

The humorous side to this event came to light later

when the building contractor for the parking terrace said, "If I'd known that President McKay was going to pray for rain when dedicating the bell tower, I'd have increased my bid to include costly delays because of water in the excavation!"

The building contractor had respect for a prophet's prayers.

Prayers are answered for the Cathys of the world as well as for the prophets.

We have discussed many aspects of life as you strive to become a special girl, a certain kind of bell-ringing, life-enriching person. I've suggested that you be a bell ringer with your friends, with boys, with your family, with people in general, and with God in particular. I promise that as you remember the symbol of the bell that rings to bring about much good, you will be happier.

Bells are wonderful!

But so are you. Go ring a few!